MW01193355

Educational Leadership and the Global Majority

Rosemary M. Campbell-Stephens

# Educational Leadership and the Global Majority

## Decolonising Narratives

palgrave
macmillan

Rosemary M. Campbell-Stephens
Visiting Fellow at the Institute of Education
University College London
London, UK

ISBN 978-3-030-88281-5          ISBN 978-3-030-88282-2    (eBook)
https://doi.org/10.1007/978-3-030-88282-2

© The Editor(s) (if applicable) and The Author(s), under exclusive licence to Springer Nature Switzerland AG 2021
This work is subject to copyright. All rights are solely and exclusively licensed by the Publisher, whether the whole or part of the material is concerned, specifically the rights of translation, reprinting, reuse of illustrations, recitation, broadcasting, reproduction on microfilms or in any other physical way, and transmission or information storage and retrieval, electronic adaptation, computer software, or by similar or dissimilar methodology now known or hereafter developed.
The use of general descriptive names, registered names, trademarks, service marks, etc. in this publication does not imply, even in the absence of a specific statement, that such names are exempt from the relevant protective laws and regulations and therefore free for general use.
The publisher, the authors and the editors are safe to assume that the advice and information in this book are believed to be true and accurate at the date of publication. Neither the publisher nor the authors or the editors give a warranty, expressed or implied, with respect to the material contained herein or for any errors or omissions that may have been made. The publisher remains neutral with regard to jurisdictional claims in published maps and institutional affiliations.

Cover pattern © Melisa Hasan

This Palgrave Macmillan imprint is published by the registered company Springer Nature Switzerland AG.
The registered company address is: Gewerbestrasse 11, 6330 Cham, Switzerland

*I dedicate this book to my mother Mary, who is an eternal gift from God; my beloved father Methuselah, who died when I was seven years old; my youngest sister Jo, now passed into ancestorhood, rest in power.*
*I dedicate this book to my dear husband William; quite simply, without his input, encouragement, challenge and love, it would have been less than it should be.*
*I also dedicate this book to all the educators with whom it has been my privilege to work alongside and serve over the years and, in particular, the exceptional team that made Investing in Diversity the pivotal catalyst for change in educational leadership development that it became.*

# Acknowledgements

I would like to acknowledge all the incredible people who have travelled with me on an educational journey that at times has been breathtaking. There are so many stories of lifetime friends with whom I went to school, and the many friends that life has gifted me since. I would like to thank my family, my teachers at Westminster Road Primary School in Handsworth, Birmingham, the Supplementary School, and The Education Project that grew out of the African Caribbean Self-Help Organisation, 104 Heathfield Road. All the grassroots community griots, teachers, students and parents in those early days of Black consciousness inspired me. The colleagues, from whom I learned much in my various mainstream roles; fellow activists and scholars, with whom I have broken bread, reasoned, conceptualised, created and executed our own brand of 'fugitive pedagogy' in clear sight, thank you, all.

To the people who mentored me, before mentoring became a thing, I would not have dared to even dream of the narratives shared in this book without your guiding wisdom. To the activists and scholars on whose shoulders and work I firmly stand, I will forever be indebted and in awe of the contribution made. To the scholars who encouraged me to write this book and to the fellow travellers who are woven into every page of every narrative, thank you. Colleagues who have become dear friends you have all contributed to this work and what will come from the writing of it. The teachers who enrolled in the Investing in Diversity leadership programme, have become a part of my life; the fellow tutors practising educere on Investing, I carry you all in my heart. The seven women who took the seven steps in Chap. 4, the legacy of what was achieved just makes my soul sing.

Continued blessings to my family, my mother, sisters, brother, sisters-in-law, nieces, nephews, aunts, uncles and cousins, and my dear husband, for the love, support, encouragement and inspiration.

I see you, and through this book I hope that we see us, more clearly.

# CONTENTS

# About the Author

**Rosemary M. Campbell-Stephens** is a veteran educator who received her professional training in England, but her breadth of experience is international. Campbell-Stephens is a visiting fellow at the Institute of Education, University College London, and a professional associate at Leeds Beckett University, but she started her teaching career as a teacher of English. Her ground-breaking leadership work as part of the UK government London Challenge Initiative in 2003–2011 was in developing a leadership preparation programme focused on increasing the numbers of Black and Asian leaders in London Schools, for the Institute of Education, University College London. Investing in Diversity became the catalyst for subsequent leadership programmes addressing under-representation of BAME leaders in the schools' sector across England. In 2009, a sister programme, Leading for Equity, was launched at the Ontario Institute for Studies in Education, University of Toronto, Canada. Campbell-Stephens frames her work through a critical race lens and describes herself as an anti-racist, Pan-African paradigm shifter. Her work is focused on the concept of the Global Majority mindset and leadership, decolonising leadership preparation, and equity and social justice in education. Publications include 'schools@onedarlington System Leadership in Practice', 'Investing in Diversity; Changing the Face (and the Heart) of Educational Leadership' and 'Ubuntu: System Leadership in Practice', and co-authored publications include 'Leading for Equity: The Investing in Diversity Approach', 'Developing the Next Generation of Black and Global Majority Leaders for London Schools', and 'Perceptions of Career Progress: The Experiences of Black and Minority Ethnic School Leaders'. Recently she co-authored a document titled 'Leading in Colour: The Urgency of Now', framed as a call to action for white leaders. She was one of the lead associates for Succession Planning and Diversity at the National College for Teaching and Leadership in England and is a former Director of the National College for School Leadership in Jamaica. She provides bespoke training and coaching internationally, including the Black and Asian Leadership Initiative to develop more Directors of Children services in the UK from Black and Asian groups, which she has been doing since 2012. Campbell-Stephens is a keynote speaker in her areas of expertise and passion, namely developing anti-racist decolonising leadership practice, equity and social justice in education, and developing the Global Majority mindset. She currently writes and delivers leadership development programmes. In 2016 Campbell-Stephens was awarded an MBE by the Queen of England for thirty-five years' service to education in the UK. She was honoured to accept the award for her activism. As a junior elder, she embraces the label 'disruptor' and is rarely in her lane.

# CHAPTER 1

# Introduction: Global Majority Decolonising Narratives

**Abstract** This chapter examines the impact of ontological racialising and socialising over time of Black, Asian and Minority Ethnic (BAME) school leaders as minorities. At a time when systemic racism globally has been thrust into sharp relief, it argues that the continued systematic racialisation and minoritisation of Black, Asian and other people of the Global Majority is a form of neo-colonialism. It examines how an invitation to address the under-representation of Black, Asian and Minority Ethnic (BAME) school leaders in London schools became a provocation to reclaim and reframe critical discourses about the role of leadership by people of the Global Majority. Aspiring leaders accepted the invitation to collectively identify as Global Majority educators, rejecting a minoritising mindset in order to confront the challenging structural experiences of being racialised within the British education system. The leadership programme Investing in Diversity was grounded in critical theory and Black liberatory movements that centred leaders as situated, conscious, thinking and knowing, intentional actors within a systemically racist system. The aim was to challenge labelling that served to divide, minoritise and subordinate to an undefined white norm, relegating identities, epistemologies and lived experiences to the margins of professional identities. The chapter explores how identifying as belonging to the Global Majority assisted in building a collective consciousness that was transformative, empowering and disruptive.

© The Author(s), under exclusive license to Springer Nature Switzerland AG 2021
R. M. Campbell-Stephens, *Educational Leadership and the Global Majority*, https://doi.org/10.1007/978-3-030-88282-2_1

**Keywords** Global Majority • Ethnic minority • Educational leadership • Minoritisation

Western theories and models of leadership alone are insufficient to empower the eighty-five per cent of people that constitute the Global Majority. The acceptance that there is a Global Majority that operates largely from theoretical foundations constructed by a privileged powerful Western minority, that have been passed on as universal normative, objective, truths, is rarely considered or challenged in professional discourse. While the scholarship about educational leadership and diversity has increased exponentially in recent years, there is insufficient in-depth study on non-Western models of leadership, especially in cities with a global student demographic. While the Black, Asian and Minority Ethnic (BAME or BME) student and to a lesser extent the teacher demographic in major cities across Britain has become more diverse, the leadership of schools has not. Addressing the under-representation of Black and Asian leaders in London schools as part of the London Challenge Initiative (2003–2011) required extending the critical discourse on leadership beyond the narrow largely theoretical narratives about representation, inclusion and diversity, to what will these diverse leaders do differently when they get there and how does leadership development prepare them to be transformational? There remains a reluctance to name systemic racism and anti-Black discrimination as contributory factors to the lack of progression and the attrition rates of Black and Asian teachers through the UK education system in spite of an established body of considerable evidence to the contrary (Coleman & Campbell-Stephens, 2010; Bhopal & Jackson, 2013; Miller, 2016; Joslyn et al., 2018; Tereshchenko et al., 2020). Systemic and institutional racism as well as discrimination on the grounds of religion, especially Islam, remains a normalised factor in the life of Black and Asian teachers and students in the UK as it does for their communities. Addressing under-representation or underachievement cannot continue to deny the enduring legacy of racism and colonialism embedded in the fabric of British society. A recent report on the employment and retention of BAME teachers in England found:

> Racism and associated inequalities are at the forefront of BAME teachers' minds in conversations about retention, not workload. Our participants highlighted how both overt and covert racism take a toll on BAME teachers' wellbeing, progression and job satisfaction. BAME teachers had the same high levels of workload as all teachers, plus an additional 'hidden workload' of coping with racism. (Tereshchenko et al., 2020)

With a population of over nine million, London is one of the largest cities in Europe and is a global city of unprecedented diversity. Yet the education system in Britain remains ill at ease with that global diversity as it pertains to race. There is ambivalence about or resistance to acknowledging how inequity, identity and diversity intersect with race. On the one hand, the system claims to promote diversity and inclusion, while on the other problematising and complicating racialisation. By essentially seeking assimilation of difference into an unracialised white norm via dishonest narratives of inclusion that deny systemic racism, the status quo remains with whiteness as the gold standard. The covert racism that often goes undetected in research but is evident through the lack of progress in recruitment and retention of Black staff indicates that some white school leaders view their school's increasing diversity as a problem rather than an opportunity, resulting in this kind of mindset prevailing to the present day,

> to increase pressure to change and for some, also impel a greater determination to conserve and to protect the values and culture perceived as indigenous. (Lumby et al., 2009)

In 2021 there remains no explicit considerations of race in leadership preparation programmes such as the National Professional Qualification for Headship (NPQH), which routinely ignores research findings on the importance of senior leaders being racially literate, especially in diverse contexts. Leadership development remains today as colour-blind, culturally tone-deaf and contemptuous of global epistemologies as it ever was. Yet, among the explicit expressions needed from all leaders is an unequivocal commitment to anti-racist, equitable and social justice praxis for which most are totally unprepared through their training. Miller (2018) argues that

> educational leaders have a moral duty to create, promote, facilitate and embed race equality within and throughout their institutions as this is

necessary to avoid the invisibilization of BME groups in leadership and further their marginalization in educational institutions.

But educational leadership and management (ELM) theorists have remained relatively uninterested in diversity (Osler, 2006). Today while the factors affecting recruitment, retention and career progression for Black and Asian teachers are more widely known through the scholarship, the findings are not informing policy or practice. There has to be racial and cultural awareness, consciousness and positionality at every level of leadership development in order to transform education systems that educate the majority. Critically, the understanding of how structural, unconscious or institutional forms of racism work to sustain racial disparity should be made explicit in leadership development, thereby enabling leaders to dismantle it.

## Global Majority

In 2003 we grasped an opportunity to create a cadre of leaders grounded in a progressive mindset of anti-racist, inclusive, culturally relevant leadership that was critically conceptualised to be disruptive. The term 'Global Majority' was coined to reject the debilitating implications of being racialised as minorities. In addition, it was then, as it is today, a more accurate descriptor of those labelled as 'ethnic minorities' or 'diverse minority communities'. We were determined that a Black-led leadership preparation programme could build solidarity across Black and Asian communities, be authentic, and be empowering in its content, language and approach. The ongoing neo-colonial project is prefaced on a culture of separation and opposition, which further marginalises diverse groups from each other. The leadership programme Investing in Diversity sought to do the opposite, by building ethical communities of practice and solidarity, and, critically, erasing the limitations of a minority mindset, cohort by cohort.

We challenged ourselves as the programme's developers to interrogate the difference that we brought and needed to bring to colour- and race-blind leadership preparation at that time (Lopez, 2021; Moorosi, 2020). I had already been an educator for twenty-three years, so any leadership programme that I would be involved in developing had to begin with disrupting, deconstructing and dismantling epistemological frameworks logged in the minds of our Black and Asian leaders. While accepting that any impact on the entrenched anti-Blackness in the system would be long term, we were pragmatic that a twelve-month period would provide sufficient time to begin a shift in cognitive models away from a subordinated and limited mindset, towards the efficacy of a Global Majority collective:

> As critical race scholars within education and leadership Alemán and Gaytán 2017; Khalil and Brown 2020; Lopez 2003; Lynn and Parker 2006; Mensah 2019; Milner 2007 continue to help understand the importance of confronting the discourse on how diversity has failed to penetrate the salience of racism in schooling, the concepts and work of anti-racist solidarity are limited. Addressing these limitations requires preliminary revelations that demonstrate how anti-racist solidarity within educational leadership can deconstruct anti-Blackness and assist in the decolonizing to denote interactions between traditional colonizing discourses and the resistance against such discourses. (Bhattacharya, 2009)

It matters how people are categorised and labelled; it matters more how people choose to label themselves. What Du Bois describes as 'double consciousness' 'always seeing oneself through the eyes of others', 'measuring one's soul by the tape of a world that looks on in amused contempt and pity' (Du Bois, 1903), is a delicate and deeply triggering subject to raise with anyone, never mind teachers. It goes to the heart of the unspoken, largely unconscious trauma of constantly seeking a sense of identity and belonging under the white gaze. This becomes even trickier in a professional space where white supremacy thrives on not seeing, naming or knowing, so in order to assimilate the Global Majority professionals limit their own internal naming and knowing of self to fit the dominant culture. But it is precisely these kinds of critical conversations, about race, being racialised and minoritised that have to be skilfully facilitated in order to maximise the efficacy of Black and other Global Majority educators. The power to categorise people into racialised hierarchical groups restrains self-consciousness and thereby alters meaning within groups who are not self-determining. Leadership is in part tied to group membership, so the groups with which leaders identify are key to their internalised sense of efficacy. If the group with which they are identified by the wider system is a racialised minority group, when in most contexts minority status denotes deficit, looked upon with 'amused contempt and pity' how does the individual find a 'better and truer self' (Du Bois, 1903) in order to effectively become, and from that position, lead?

'Global Majority' is a constructivist term that not only confirms membership of the numerical majority on the planet, but, more importantly, moves towards reclaiming the autonomy and efficacy that the process of racialised categorisation and minoritisation removes. It raises the metaphorical ceiling on what is possible from a Global Majority perspective. First and foremost, it speaks to those labelled 'minorities' and encourages them to reject the labelling as a form of colonising the mind through erasure of memory and minoritisation. 'Global Majority' was intentionally used instead of 'minority ethnic' to shift those practitioners so labelled towards understanding themselves as having history, agency and knowledge that predates their marginalisation. They have agency in their own right as individuals and collectively as groups. Identifying contemporary concerns that intersect group divisions as part of a Global Majority significantly strengthens advocacy. To speak from a Global Majority perspective is not only to reject the neo-colonial hierarchy imposed through racialisation, but to challenge individualism regarded as the second most important feature of modernism. In addition, as critical race scholars stress (DeCuir & Dixson, 2004; Delgado & Stefancic, 2017; Ladson-Billings & Tate, 2006; Solorzano & Yosso, 2001), no single social identifier will ever erase differences, and this is not the intention here. The term Global Majority does not essentialise either the individual, the groups that make up the collective or the collective itself. The term 'Global Majority' invites social cooperation across groups, existentially to address the mutual interests of the majority on planet earth through collective mobilisation. The intention was to start that movement in school leadership preparation in London, which we did in 2003; its contemporary relevance in 2021 as we negotiate a new normal in a Covid world where Black lives strive to matter speaks for itself.

## GLOBAL PARADIGMS

In 2021, the social, political, environmental, cultural and economic structures in the current world order are imploding. In Gramscian terms,

> there has been a fundamental breakdown in the equilibrium of social structures whose peak is at an impasse: as the group holding this structure together is falling apart, no other political force is viable enough to take over. (Bates, 1975)

This has led to an urgent need for a post-structuralist radical paradigm shift, moving at pace towards alternative social, cultural and economic structures. Solutions to these challenges may present for example in the form of collective leadership across traditional group boundaries, bound together by a central set of values around which these groups can cohere—values such as the ancient Egyptian ethical model of Maat, which has varied meanings but centres truth, justice, propriety, balance, harmony, reciprocity and order. The collective response requires cooperation at the scales commensurate with the challenge; hence the need for the Global Majority to move beyond being a numerical fact to a system that centres the needs of the majority in practice and draws on a range of traditional global ways of navigating a globalised, technical modern world, that still needs to address, ethics, order, morality and the nature of what it is to be human:

> It is in this meaning as natural and moral law and order that Maat has parallels with other foundational worldview principles in various other religious and ethical traditions such as cieng, in the Dinka tradition (Deng 1972), Rta in the Hindu tradition (Singh 1984), dike in the Homeric Greek tradition (Tobin 1987), and tao in the Chinese tradition (Tu 1985). However, none of these parallel concepts is as all-embracing in its conception and function as Maat is in the ancient Egyptian ethical tradition. In the Dinka tradition, cieng is, at its core, a moral-order concept and principle which means, as a verb, 'to live together, to look after, to order or put in order, etc.' (Deng 1972, 13). And as a noun, 'it means morals, behavior, habit, conduct, and the nature of custom, rule, law, way of life and culture'. (Karenga, 2004)

The term 'Global Majority' includes those people who identify as Black, African, Asian, Brown, Arab and mixed heritage, are indigenous to the global south, and/or have been racialised as 'ethnic minorities'. Globally, these groups currently represent approximately eighty-five per cent of the world's population, making them the Global Majority now. With current growth rates, notwithstanding the Covid-19 virus and its emerging variants, they are set to remain the Global Majority into the foreseeable future. Understanding that singular truth may shift the dial: it certainly should permanently disrupt and relocate conversations about minorities and draw some attention to those maintaining outdated categorisations and their motivations for doing so. The 'logic', for example, of talking about majority/minority cities in the USA begs many questions.

The way in which the development programme initially worked was to acknowledge the diversity and knowledge, of the leader. Secondly, to provide a space for Global Majority educators to be able to self-identify and come to terms with their individual and professional identity, not regardless of who they were, but with due regard to all of those multi-layered facets of who they *are*. Learning to be, means opening up to different ways of knowing and being.

To have the intellectual space to deconstruct the nature of the racialised system in which they work and understand how systemically inequitable practices are engrained and normalised within routine processes was a critical part of the development process. The seduction of an inclusionist, assimilating agenda focused on representation alone had to be resisted as essentially this did little more than train Black and Asian aspirant leaders to navigate the leadership space on tiptoe, unchanged by their presence. The only ethical position was to bring disruption to a schooling system, that had been relentless in arresting the development of Black and other Global Majority communities for generations. The training invited explorations of more indigenous ways of leading around those centred questions of ethics, race, indigeneity, service and spirituality, and their intersections with social justice and social equity work (Gooden & Dantley, 2012). It was never about fitting into the existing space, although this would have been less problematic for the system; it had to be about changing that space or creating an alternative. Many participants went on to creatively do one if not both of those two things, change the space or create an alternative, but not before the personal cognitive reset from minority to majority, which for many took several years.

I have therefore intentionally used the term 'Global Majority' since 2003, when I was invited, or more accurately invited myself, to develop a leadership programme for 'ethnic minority' teachers in London schools, which we called 'Investing in Diversity' (Johnson & Campbell-Stephens, 2012). I wanted to trouble a Eurocentric colonial mentality that racialised and minoritised as if that were the only way of collectively categorising Black and Asian teachers within the London context:

> The term 'racially-minoritised', attributed to Yasmin Gunaratnum in 2003, provides a social constructionist approach to understanding that others actively minoritise people, rather than people naturally existing as minorities or ethnic minorities, implying minority, as racial. (Gunaratnam, 2003)

The intention was to bring that trouble both to the systemic consequences of such labelling as well as to Global Majority leaders in the making and the way in which their internalised labelling could hold them back. The concern existed at two levels. First, the continued use of terms such as 'ethnic minority' relegated the Black, Asian, African and African Caribbean educators' skills, knowledge, theories, models, ways of being and lived experiences to the margins of any discourse on leadership, because they were 'minorities' (Ramaioli, 2021). Second, we wanted to attract aspirant leaders who were unambivalent about their identity and did not think of themselves as 'ethnic minorities'. We sought aspiring leaders who already had high levels of racial affinity and comfort, were ethnically and culturally literate, and were confident enough to work with and learn from other Global Majority groups in contexts where the student demographic placed them in the majority and the position of providing service.

To address the concern of homogenisation, there was never any intention through the use of the term Global Majority to dismiss the ethnic and racial categories with which people identify, such as Black, Asian, dual-heritage or indigenous, quite the opposite: the Investing in Diversity programme celebrated difference as enriching and worthy of investment (Campbell-Stephens, 2009; Portelli & Campbell-Stephens, 2009). The programme was predicated on inviting, acknowledging and amplifying the voices of aspiring school leaders from diverse backgrounds to find their authentic best self. In addition, the intersectionality theory attributed to scholars such as Kimberlé Crenshaw and Patricia Hill Collins, and the power dynamics which include contradictions and challenges connected with race, as well as the intersections across class, gender, socio-economic status, religion, disability and sexuality were all fully accepted. People live multiple and layered identities.

Global Majority conceptualisation categorically rejects the subordinate status of ethnic minority and the centring of whiteness as the norm. Instead, it embraces the independence, potential interdependence and connectedness of diverse communities who together make up the Global Majority. The concept de-problematises human diversity. It accepts that multiple ways of knowing and being, including complexity and fluidity within and across groups, can and do co-exist. It provides a majority wide lens through which to view what are global matters. In the case of school leadership, it strengthens the capacity of the peoples of the Global Majority to work with each other and alongside white colleagues, on the kind of equal footing that they do not have as ethnic minorities. It presents an opportunity to acknowledge their differences as assets rather than additional ways of 'othering', assets that can make a difference to all of the diverse communities that schools in London serve.

For the people of the Global Majority, being a numerical majority is not enough. They have to reclaim the power and authority that comes with their numerical advantage to take on their responsibility as a new world order emerges and rediscover epistemologies of their own. The concept Global Majority goes some way towards the psychological cognitive resetting work required to become people with both a decolonised global and a majority mindset. By challenging the notion that whiteness is the global norm, the intention is to permanently reframe conversations about race, equity, community and leadership, from a majority, post-colonial mindset, and thereby contribute to the task of decolonisation of which so much has been written (Fanon, 1963; Abdi, 2011; Quijano, 2007; Simmons & Dei, 2012; Lopez, 2021).

Both disruption and precision were required in the discourse on school leadership in London in 2003; not all minoritised groups were experiencing the system in the same way. The assumed majority perspective remained staunchly white, Western and stubbornly colour-blind at a time when the student demographic in London, like most major cities in the West, was moving rapidly in the opposite direction. London's 2021 population is estimated at 9,221,300 according to London Datastore; the census results for 2021 have not yet been released. There are 330 languages spoken in London and while it is difficult to get exact figures from the way the data sets are now collated, the London boroughs with the highest numbers of ethnic minority school age populations upwards of fifty per cent, include Lambeth, Southwark, Lewisham, Croydon, Newham, Brent, Hackney, Enfield, Greenwich, Redbridge, Haringey, Waltham Forest, Barking and Dagenham, Tower Hamlets, Harrow, Ealing, Hounslow and Hillingdon, over half of the thirty-two London boroughs. Seventy-three per cent of students across London are young people of the Global Majority.

## From BAME to Global Majority

The normalisation of systemic racism meant that we had reached a critical inflection point. While a Black and Global Majority epistemology in educational leadership was definitely required, it had to be approached with caution, so first steps in that direction were necessarily modest. The team understood that many BAME educators in the UK were conflicted about various things, including their identity. Bespoke leadership preparation that was focused on them and on formulating an alternative Black perspective could present risk and unwanted exposure for those of an assimilationist predisposition. The situation was not helped by some researchers and commentators conflating culturally and contextually responsive professional development that acknowledged the systemic racism demonstrated by their own research, with concerns about preferential treatment and Positive Action. The irony is that in Britain, Positive Action is more of a myth than a reality in practice. However, like the current media storms about Critical Race Theory, culture wars and the cancel culture rhetoric, the threat that so-called Positive Action initiatives might pose to the schooling system was amplified by the media to a fever-pitch level. Consequentially, some Black educators resisted bespoke training because of the perception that it was giving them an unfair advantage or, more importantly, would be unsettling for their white colleagues and ultimately challenging the dominating culture. Policymakers talked glibly about it taking another fifty years for Black students to catch up with their counterparts, and a little more of your soul died, as you realised that you didn't have another fifty years and it was your great grandchildren that they were talking about.

Educational research in the last thirty years on students' achievement has identified the quality of school leadership as one of the key determiners of student outcomes (Leithwood & Hallinger, 2002). While some research examined the importance of difference in context and the impact of globalisation for example, there was up until recently a paucity of research that moved beyond leadership traits, dispositions, competences and models as if these were somehow abstract, objective, neutral activities separate from (a) who the leader is and (b) the level of cultural competence that the leader has by virtue of their ethnicity, especially when leading in diverse contexts (Lopez, 2021; Miller, 2019; Smith, 2021).

In contrast, considerable amounts of irrefutable data through research and reports continue to accumulate that indicate against a background of improved achievement overall the widening achievement gap between white and Black students that is contributing to third, and fourth-generation Black students being failed in British schools (Coard, 1971; Stone, 1981; Rampton, 1981; Swann, 1985; Blair et al., 1998; Macpherson, 1999; Gillborn & Mirza, 2000; GLA, 2004; Demie, 2015, 2021). Critically, the same student groups that were being failed by the system were being over-represented in exclusions, managed moves, Pupil Referral Units (PRUs) and Alternative Provision, as well as falling vulnerable to the criminal justice system and feeding the school-to-prison pipeline (Institute for Public Policy Research, 2017, Timpson Review, 2019, Institute of Race Relations, 2020). What is particularly reprehensible is that there are large educational organisations who while selling their educational programmes to regions in the global south, erase from their reports any reference to race, preferring to talk about 'distinctive and complex ethnic profile' and only referencing underachievement as it relates to 'disadvantaged students' (identifiable in national data in the UK as those pupils receiving Free School Meals). Acknowledging how race and class impact education is critical in understanding the inequities that continue to plague our education systems. It is essential for leaders and leadership preparation programmes to specifically address race when understanding disproportionality in teaching and learning, systems, structures and policies that continue to widen the gap specifically for Black and other racialised students.

The under-representation of school leaders that reflect the communities that they serve continues (Bush et al., 2006; Coleman & Campbell-Stephens, 2009; Lumby & Morrison, 2010; Pierre & Mboyo, 2017; Miller, 2014, 2016, 2019). The privatisation of education via academisation and free schools is having little impact either on diversifying school leadership or on narrowing the most stubborn attainment gaps (Gillborn and Youdell, 2000). In addition, some communities have concerns about already high levels of exclusions being even higher in some academy chains.

There had been back in 2003 modest focus on diversifying leaders or different kinds of leadership but a stubborn resistance to focus on teachers and leaders from different ethnic and racial backgrounds. There was no government-funded large-scale initiative focused on recruiting and retaining Black and Asian school leaders until London Challenge and Investing in Diversity (IiD) in 2003, and the subsequent diversity programmes that it was the forerunner for across the country outside of London. The programmes outside of London, such as Diverse Leaders for Tomorrow in Yorkshire and Humber, were funded by the National College for Teaching and Leadership and then directly by the Department for Education up until 2013, when the department shifted its focus to other areas of inequity. Again, tellingly, there is no official reference to these bespoke programmes in any government reports.

The Global Majority movement recognises legacy and was intentional in connecting Black and Asian teachers to the legacies of intellectualism, resistance, struggle and activism on which they were knowingly or unknowingly building globally or specifically in the UK. To do less than recognise the shoulders on which we stand is, as the actress Lupita Nyong'o said is tantamount to 'witchcraft'. Black educators who started teaching in the 1970s and 1980s as I did would have been oriented in our identities by community resistance to racism which was widespread in the UK. Black conscious community resistance dating from the early 1960s through the 1990s, would include but are not limited to:

- Black Parents Movements (Black Cultural Archives, George Padmore Institute)
- Caribbean Teachers Associations (The National Archives)
- ILEA (the Inner London Education Authority)
- Black sections of Teachers Unions within the NUT (National Union of Teachers) and later the NASUWT (National Association of School Masters Union of Women Teachers).
- African Caribbean Supplementary Community Saturday Schools (National Association of Black Supplementary Schools)
- National Antiracist Movement in Education (George Padmore Institute)
- Black publishers such as Bogle L'Ouverture Publishing House and New Beacon Books; the International Book Fair of Radical Black and Third World Books (1982–1995)
- London Schools and the Black Child (2003–2014, Diane Abbott)
- Education and The Black Child Conferences held outside of London (1993–1997, Kemetic Education Guidance)
- Afrikan Liberation Day annual conferences (1970s ongoing)
- Community Empowerment Network (Gus John)

We sought in Investing in Diversity to reconnect or in many cases connect for the first time Black and Asian teachers with that legacy of resistance to racism through organised action, that history of self-determination through the establishment of Supplementary schools, to reassure them that they were not starting from scratch, as individual 'ethnic minorities' unconnected to self, memory or community, but that each generation had its work to do. The Investing in Diversity programme was organised over a twelve-month period, beginning with a residential weekend and followed by ten after school or 'twilight' sessions and a whole-day seminar at the end of the year. Every residential weekend began with a keynote address presented by Professor Gus John, the first Black Director of Education in the country, and a long-time African Caribbean community activist who has been at the forefront of equal rights and racial politics in Britain for more than thirty years (John, 2006). Contemporary research in the USA is far more forthright in acknowledging the vital role that Black teachers play in supporting, not just the achievement of Black students but their wellbeing, than similar research in the UK (Dantley & Tillman, 2006). This is where Black and other Global Majority professionals work twice as hard in the UK, not by trying to prove themselves as equal to their white counterparts, but by throwing their hearts, minds, souls and bodies in the way of protecting Black students from a soul-destroying curriculum, low teacher expectations, biased assessments, punitive setting, heavy-handed behaviour management from a very early age, the micro-aggressions on hair, culture, and ultimately exclusion, and the morally bankrupt school-to-prison pipeline.

The concluding chapter will reflect on contemporary content for a global programme, but suffice to say here, Investing in Diversity had to explicitly address the Global Majority leader's and teacher's roles in stemming the worst excesses of systemic and institutional racism on Black and Brown children's lives. For them it was not an academic exercise (Elonga Mboyo, 2019).

## CONCLUSION

Investing in Diversity encouraged African and Asian people to connect with their cultural identities and communities, as part of their professional identities and provide contextually appropriate culturally responsive leadership. It sought to encourage personal growth by expecting an investment by those on the programme in acquiring cultural knowledge and indigenous understanding of the narratives of their individual communities' struggles. The programme required a level of understanding of the differential and devious way in which systemic racism worked. Emphasis was placed on building community across ethnic and cultural boundaries.

The concept Global Majority also speaks to a new global possibility, a diasporic identity, that does not seek to dominate, erase or enforce a hierarchy. Within the term, diversity is acknowledged, embraced, confronted, particularly the internal power dynamics within groups and occasionally celebrated when the potential collective agency is realised. It is aspirational about a different kind of interdependence, but not naive. The concept of being part of a Global Majority is in part understanding that we have been racialised, divided, placed in hierarchies, made oppositional to one another, and that in some instances these divisions have been self-inflicted and internalised. Moving away from the Black and white binary, it is time to explore those deeply challenging areas and, for example, trouble the complicity with white supremacy of some Brown colleagues racialised as the model minority, as well as 'non-white' colleagues who do not consider themselves Black (Brown complicity in White supremacy, 2020).

So, within the term 'Global Majority' there is the acceptance of a need to resolve the tension of the politics of naming, particularly in this instance of educational leadership and representation. Global Majority provides an alternative to other collective terms such as Black and Minority Ethnic, Visible Minority or People of Colour. However, it does not in any way preclude different groups from naming their identities, including 'race', and it allows for some fluidity across old, fixed demarcation lines that have become irrelevant in identity. We accept that addressing physical representations of varied bodies in educational leadership requires naming. What it does remove, however, is the implied subordination to a white never defined aggressive norm. The challenge becomes for the Global Majority to confidently confront the differential negative impact of systems and structures on the majority, and begin to construct a collective mindset, conversation and focus that centres the social interests of the majority.

The Global Majority term and concept remains aspirational and intentional. The aim is that solidarity across the educational communities of the global south can be built and that an alternative decolonial epistemology that deconstructs and dismantles the remnants of the colonial education systems, that continue to arrest development in developing countries and wherever the diaspora is located, including in the cities of the developed world can be. Global circumstances now require alternative modalities moving with urgency towards life, equity and wellbeing, a globality focused on the need of the majority. This brings inevitable new challenges such as

a hubristic Eurocentric conviction that only European history and knowledge informs the natural and the universal because (western) modernity is supposedly the only blueprint which leads to developed, modern, and civilized status. Development according to Western modernization theory is solely attained by peoples adopting western contours of civilization such as Liberalism and Capitalism. (Al-Kassimi, 2018)

I subscribe to the conviction that in 2021 humanity can find common ground, empathy for the conditions of the majority, solidarity around a set of values, a purpose, a destination around which we can cohere, a different type of globalisation, if you will. There are already examples of the global south seeking to reimagine and collaborate on development, economics and culture. Sometimes it proves easier to arrive at consensus about what we are against, than about what we are collectively for, but the destination is worth the effort of the journey. Global interdependence, collective action, different perspectives, looking to each other for innovative ideas and models culturally appropriate and relevant to context, in relation to specific issues, will define the new world order for the majority.

So, perhaps now is the time for the Global Majority, when most former colonies have had at least six or seven decades of 'independence', to cooperate in finding current common causes around which they can unite. Education could be that common ground, and the confronting of a number of pressing issues. Firstly, the changed world following two significant global events: the Coronavirus pandemic and Black Lives Matter foregrounding the human rights of Black people. Combined they expose inequity and bring new vitality to the conversations about decolonisation and the role of education now. Education in a Covid-19 world presents many challenges, but also a new global opportunity to fundamentally reimagine the purpose of education. A schooling system predicated on the majority failing, that has its roots firmly in the utilitarian purpose of providing a basic education to produce a compliant workforce with low level skills for the workplace, that refuses to see the majority, except as cheap labour or a commodity is not what developing countries of the global south need from their education systems now. Could seeking consensus on educational purpose in a Global Majority focused world provide the focus for a third Bandung conference?

The first Bandung (Asian-African) conference took place in 1955. Its core principles were political self-determination, mutual respect for sovereignty, non-aggression, non-interference in internal affairs, and equality. Most of the attendant leaders had recently emerged from colonial rule, and Africa was under-represented because so many countries had yet to achieve independence and had been advised not to attend by their colonial masters. The objectives agreed to at the close of the conference are still salient today: economic and cultural cooperation, the protection of human rights and the principle of self-determination, an end to racial discrimination and peaceful coexistence. In 2005 on the 50th anniversary of the original conference, Asian and African leaders met again, this time in Jakarta, to launch the New Asian-African Strategic Partnership (NAASP) to promote political, economic and cultural cooperation between the two continents.

The focus of this book will in the main be on the Black, African and African Caribbean contingent of the peoples that together constitute the Global Majority not for any reason of considering them more important than other Global Majority communities. They are all matters of practicality and what can be developed within the boundaries of this publication. The focus, too, speaks to my area of expertise, but there is also something about the particular role that Africa and Africans have played and continue to play in the world and the particular form of parasitic colonisation that has been visited on this part of the Global Majority which warrants more detailed study. The devastation of the Maafa (African Holocaust) on Africans globally cannot be overstated and has no equivalent. The dehumanising process, the displacement of peoples, subordination to the point of eradication of languages and religion and their continued persecution through neo-colonialism and neo-capitalism over centuries is unparalleled. The extent to which former colonisers continue to immorally destroy Africans on the continent and her people in the diaspora, while taking her land, resources and relying on the continent to contribute through colonial taxes and indenture through debt to the wealth of their nations, is again without comparison to any other group. Critically, there has been no truth-telling by the perpetrators of these crimes against African humanity over centuries, no reconciliation, no reparations just continued subjugation and an eradicating of the evidence of what has been done and is being done.

When the continent with a larger footprint than China, India, Europe and the USA combined ceases to be referred to as it was on my last international flight by the flight attendant collecting funds for charity as one of the 'countries' that she has worked in, then we know that some progress will have been made towards this part of the Global Majority being afforded the respect and recognition that they deserve.

The Global Majority concept and the leadership development model that it birthed contributes not just to the discourse on leadership and decolonisation, but a new form of globalisation or globality, not based on feeding the economic greed of the minority, but one based on addressing the human need of the majority beginning with decolonised humanising education systems across the globe.

REFERENCES

Abdi, A. (2011). *Decolonizing philosphies of education*. Sense Publishers.

Al-Kassimi, K. (2018). ALBA: A decolonial delinking performance towards (western) modernity – An alternative to development project. *Cogent Social Sciences, 4*, 1546418.

The first large-scale Asian–African or Afro–Asian Conference – Also known as the Bandung Conference (Indonesian: *Konferensi Asia-Afrika*) – Was a meeting of Asian and African states, most of which were newly independent, which took place on 18–24 April 1955 in Bandung, West Java, Indonesia.

Bates, T. (1975). Gramsci and the theory of hegemony. *Journal of the History of Ideas, 36*(2), 351–366. https://doi.org/10.2307/2708933

Bhattacharya K. (2009). Othering Research, Researching the Other: De/Colonizing Approaches to Qualitative Inquiry. In j. C. Smart (Eds.) *Higher Education: Handbook of Theory and Research*, 24. Springer: Dordrecht. https://doi.org/10.1007/978-1-4020-9628-0_3

Bhopal, K., & Jackson, J. (2013). *The experiences of black and minority ethnic academics: Multiple identities and career progression* (29pp). University of Southampton.

Blair, M., & Bourne, J., with Coffin, C., Creese, A., & Kenner, C. (1998). *Making the difference: Teaching and learning strategies in successful multi-ethnic schools*. Department for Education and Employment.

Brown complicity in White supremacy: Towards solidarity with Black lives. (2020, June 19). https://youtu.be/LmaVUiEjb0o

Bush, T., Glover, D., & Sood, K. (2006). Black and minority ethnic leaders in England: A portrait. *School Leadership and Management, 26*(3), 289–305.

Campbell-Stephens, R. (2009). Investing in diversity; changing the face (and the heart) of educational leadership. *School Leadership and Management, 29*(3), 321–331.

Coard, B. (1971). *How the West Indian child is made educationally subnormal in the British school system*. New Beacon Books.

Coleman, M., & Campbell-Stephens, R. (2009). *Progress to school leadership: Experiences of Black and Minority Ethnic (BME) senior staff*. Occasional Paper 9, WLE Centre, Institute of Education, London.

Coleman, M., & Campbell-Stephens, R. (2010). Perceptions of career progress: The experience of black and minority ethnic school leaders. *School Leadership and Management, 30*(1), 35–49.

Dantley, M. E., & Tillman, L. C. (2006). Social justice and moral transformative leadership. In C. Marshall & M. Oliva (Eds.), *Leadership for social justice: Making revolutions in education* (pp. 16–30). Pearson.

DeCuir, J., & Dixson, J. (2004). "So when it comes out, they aren't that surprised that it is there": Using critical race theory as a tool of analysis of race and racism in education. *Educational Researcher, 33*(5), 26–31.

Delgado, R., & Stefancic, J. (2017). *Critical race theory* (3rd ed.). New York University Press. https://doi.org/10.18574/9781479851393

Demie, F. (2015). *The underachievement of Black Caribbean heritage pupils in schools*. Research Brief. Lambeth Schools Research and Statistics Unit.

Demie, F. (2021). The experience of Black Caribbean pupils in school exclusion in England. *Education Review, 73*(1), 55–70.

Du Bois, W. E. (1903). *The souls of Black folk*. A.C. McClurg and Co., Chicago.

Elonga Mboyo, J. P. (2019). School leadership and Black and minority ethnic career prospects in England: The choice between being a group prototype or deviant head teacher. *Educational Management Administration and Leadership, 47*(1), 110–128.

Fanon, F. (1963). *The wretched of the earth* (C. Farrington, Trans.). Grove Press.

Gillborn, D., & Mirza, H. S. (2000). *Educational inequality: Mapping race and class*. OfSTED.

Gillborn, D., & Youdell, D. (2000). *Rationing education: Policy, practice, reform and equity*. Open University Press.

GLA. (2004). *The educational experiences and achievement of Black boys in London schools 2000–2003*. London Development Agency, Greater London Authority.

Gooden, M., & Dantley, M. (2012). Centering race in framework for leadership preparation. *Journal of Research on Leadership Education, 7*(2), 237–253.

Gunaratnam, Y. (2003). *Researching 'race' and ethnicity: Methods, knowledge and power*. Sage.

Institute for Public Policy Research. (2017, October). *Making the difference: Breaking the link between school exclusion and social exclusion*. Retrieved October, 2017, from https://www.ippr.org/files/2017-10/making-the-difference-report-october-2017.pdf

Institute of Race Relations. (2020). *How Black working-class youth are criminalised and excluded in the English school system: A London case study*.

John, G. (2006). *Taking a stand: Gus John speaks on education, race, social action and civil unrest 1980–2005*. Gus John Partnership.

Johnson, L., & Campbell-Stephens, R. (2012). Developing the next generation of Black and global majority leaders for London schools. *Journal of Educational Administration, 51*(1), 24–39.

Joslyn, E., Miller, P., & Callender, C. (2018). Leadership and diversity in education in England: Progress in the new millennium? Belmas Paper. *Management in Education, 32*(4), 149–151.

Karenga, M. (2004). *Maat: The moral ideal in ancient Egypt*. Los Angeles: University of Sankore Press.

Ladson-Billings, G., & Tate, W. (2006). *Education research in the public interest: Social justice, action, and policy.* Teachers College Press.

Leithwood, K., & Hallinger, P. (2002). *Second international handbook of educational leadership and administration.* Kluwer Academic Publishers.

Lopez, A. E. (2021). Examining alternative school leadership practices and approaches: A decolonising school leadership approach. *Intercultural Education.* https://doi.org/10.1080/14675986.2021.1889471

Lumby, J., & Morrison, M. (2010). Leadership and diversity: Theory and research. *School Leadership and Management, 1*(30), 3–17.

Lumby, J., Crow, G., & Pashiardis, P. (2009). *International handbook on the preparation and development of school leaders.* Routledge.

Macpherson, W. (1999). *The Stephen Lawrence inquiry.* CM 4262-I. The Stationery Office.

Miller, P. (2014). Becoming a principal: Exploring perceived discriminatory practices in the appointment and selection of principals in Jamaica and England. In K. Beycioglu & P. Pashiardis (Eds.), *Multidimensional perspectives on principal leadership effectiveness* (pp. 132–147). IGI Global.

Miller, P. (2016). 'White sanction', institutional, group and individual interaction in the promotion and progression of black and minority ethnic academics and teachers in England. *Power and Education, 8*(3), 205–221.

Miller, P. W. (2018). The nature of school leadership. In *The nature of school leadership. Intercultural studies in education.* Palgrave Macmillan. https://doi.org/10.1007/978-3-319-70105-9_9

Miller, P. (2019). 'Tackling' race inequality in school leadership: Positive actions in BAME teacher progression – Evidence from three English schools. *Educational Management Administration and Leadership 2020, 48*(6), 986–1006.

Moorosi, P. (2020). Colour-blind educational leadership policy: A critical race theory analysis of school principalship standards in South Africa. *Educational Management Administration and Leadership 2021, 49*(4), 644–661.

Osler, A. (2006). Excluded girls: Interpersonal, institutional and structural violence in schooling. *Gender and Education, 18*(6), 571–589. https://doi.org/10.1080/09540250600980089

Pierre, J., & Mboyo, E. (2017). Reimagining Ubuntu in schools: A perspective from two primary school leaders in the Democratic Republic of Congo. *Educational Management Administration & Leadership 2019, 47*(2), 206–223.

Portelli, J. P., & Campbell-Stephens, R. (2009). *Leading for equity: The investing in diversity approach.* Edphil Books.

Quijano, A. (2007). Coloniality and modernity/rationality. *Cultural Studies, 21*(2–3), 168–178. https://doi.org/10.1080/09502380601164353

Ramaioli, M. (2021). The making of a minority: Subalternity and minoritisation of Jordanian Salafism. In P. Maggiolini & I. Ouahes (Eds.), *Minorities and state-*

*building in the Middle East. Minorities in West Asia and North Africa.* Palgrave Macmillan. https://doi.org/10.1007/978-3-030-54399-0_9

Rampton, A. (1981). *West Indian children in our schools.* Cmnd 8273. HMSO.

Simmons, M., & Dei, G. (2012). Reframing anti-colonial theory for the diasporic context. *Postcolonial Directions in Education, 1*(1), 67–99. OISE University of Toronto.

Smith, P. (2021). Black male school leaders: Protectors and defenders of children, community, culture, and village. *Journal of School Leadership 2021, 31*(1–2), 29–49. Sage.

Solorzano, D., & Yosso, T. (2001). From racial stereotyping and deficit discourse toward a critical race theory in teacher education. *Multicultural Education, 9*(1, Fall), 2–8.

Stone, M. (1981). *The education of the Black child in Britain, the myth of multiracial education.* Fontana.

Swann, L. (1985). *Education for all: Final report of the Committee of Inquiry into the education of children from ethnic minority groups.* Cmnd 9453. HMSO.

Tereshchenko, A., Mills, M., & Bradbury, A. (2020). *Making progress? Employment and retention of BAME teachers in England.* UCL Institute of Education.

Timpson Review of School Exclusion, Parliament Paper. (2019, May). https://assets.publishing.service.gov.uk/government/uploads/system/uploads/attachment_data/file/807862/Timpson_review.pdf

# Process of Racialisation, Creation of a Single Narrative and Restoration of Memory

**Abstract** This chapter challenges the ontology of a single definitive narrative on race through a systematic process of racialisation over centuries. It examines the roots, methods and occasionally the detail of domination through erasure and the construction of a detrimentally powerful alternative narrative of Africa as the dark continent. It explores the global social events that have over time consolidated the categorisation of racialised people. Using the awareness that colonisation is anything dominating or imposing (Dei, *Canadian Review of Sociology, 33*(3), 247–267, 1996; Kempf & Moizeau, *Journal of Public Economic Theory, 11*(4), 529–564, 2009), the chapter confronts how indigenous peoples of the Global Majority have been dehumanised often in pursuit of profit. It specifically examines the impact of othering Africa and African people within global discourse and demonstrates how a restoration of memory can create new meaning and essential knowledge.

**Keywords** Racialisation • Colonisation • Minoritisation • Dehumanisation

© The Author(s), under exclusive license to Springer Nature Switzerland AG 2021
R. M. Campbell-Stephens, *Educational Leadership and the Global Majority*, https://doi.org/10.1007/978-3-030-88282-2_2

## RACIALISATION

My experience of being racialised has been uneven. Being positively racialised as Black from birth, reinforced within my Jamaican family through my upbringing and my primary school years left me firmly grounded in a positive sense of identity. Whiteness while present was not for me the norm. My world, even at seven years of age was bigger than the street and the lovely home in which I grew up. I was definitely situated in that world, not as an observer, but as an active participant. Making my own meaning, writing my own stories, being of consequence, having opinions, being seen, heard and listened to was all normal. I was aware of white people, I loved some of them, because they were my Primary school teachers, but whiteness was not at the centre of my consciousness and at that time it was inconsequential to my identity. This 'racial' pride placed me in good stead for my subsequent Grammar school and University experiences of being racialised, which were entirely different to that of my earlier formative years. In this world, whiteness functioned as the norm and whiteness's power was dependent on racialising me as Black. Expectations of teachers and lecturers through my secondary education and while training to teach were not as high and had more detrimental consequences. I was conscious of not now being seen or heard, becoming irrelevant, or conversely being either overly exposed, or under surveillance, which was more problematic, because then you are viewed as a threat to the status quo. While training to teach, I remember what could be described as two tipping point moments, the first was when in discussion with one of my lecturers I suggested that I compare and contrast the Jamaican poet Louise Bennett's and English poet Wilfred Owen's take on the futility of war. His reaction while interested was to say, 'but there is nobody here to supervise this.' I was disappointed that he had not grasped the opportunity to learn something from one of his students, audacious of me some may even say arrogant. I now realise that I hadn't fully grasped the concept of white fragility, and while my understanding of white power was becoming embedded, I did not yet perceive of myself as a threat.

In addition, I was struck by the realisation that I actually didn't wish to be 'supervised', not in this particular instance. I hoped that some other kind of liberatory agreement or understanding could be entered into between teacher and student, at least for that assignment, in that moment. The limitations of the Russell Group University space were beginning to be exposed, as was its incapacity to do what my Junior school had done so effectively, namely *educere* to bring out, rather than *educare* to put in:

> Education either functions as an instrument which is used to facilitate integration of the younger generation into the logic of the present system and bring about conformity or it becomes the practice of freedom, the means by which men and women deal critically and creatively with reality and discover how to participate in the transformation of their world. (Freire, 1970)

The next tipping-point moment was when on leaving the University, the same lecturer offered me some unsolicited advice namely, he suggested that I, 'might wish to re-consider my involvement with the Afro-Caribbean organisation' with which I was by now intimately involved. Here my Blackness was in confrontation with not only his individual whiteness, fragile or not, but his 'advice' that carried the full authority of the white system which could crush you. He was right, I did reconsider and re-arranged my life so that for the next eight years I could, while being a full-time teacher of English, then an advisory teacher, before becoming a too young Ofsted Inspector, three different roles in three different cities, co-run that Pan-African Saturday Community school at which I used to volunteer. I soon came to realise that being a conscious Black practitioner in predominantly white contexts often meant being towards the bottom of or completely outside of an opaque, ill-defined hierarchy, while somehow simultaneously requiring surveillance. When the situation was confronted, which I periodically elected not to do, the territory was psychologically stressful, depressing and draining of energy. I could see how some Black people being in a minority situation might locate the source of that stress in being Black, instead of understanding that it was the meaning that being under the white gaze brought to being racialised Black, the opposition and perceived threat that being Black posed to whiteness, that was the source of the stress.

## IDENTITY

I was confronted by the impact of such racialisation on groups of African and Asian aspiring school leaders in London in 2003. By then, I was acutely aware that the process of racialisation, for the individual as well as the collective can have devastating impacts on how people identify and turn up or not in the world personally and professionally (Selvarajah et al,

2020). I remember the shock of reading application forms for the leadership preparation programme 'Investing in Diversity' that we had created for Black and Asian teachers and finding that some applicants had created a new category for themselves, 'non-white'. Part of the reason that we developed the leadership programme was to support a cadre of leaders who would be transformational in addressing the systemic racism that was arresting the development of so many Black and Brown students in London schools. Could people who defined themselves in terms of what they were not, instead of who they were, be the kind of transformational leaders that our system needed? The development of the Global Majority concept in 2003 in the UK was specifically about encouraging African and Asian educators in London to embrace their ethnic and cultural identities as assets, and in addition collectively identify and build solidarity with each other and other racialised groups as part of the Global Majority (Portelli & Campbell-Stephens 2009). In doing so we were challenging the kind of colonisation where whiteness functions as the norm. More of what happened, in Chap. 6. So, for the purpose of this chapter, I am seeking to more fully understand the process of racialisation by examining it in some detail, primarily because the concept is based on the idea that the object of study should not be 'race' itself, but the process by which it becomes meaningful in a particular context, had I realised this back in the 1980s when I first started out, I may have situated myself slightly differently.

It is this book's contention that while racialisation as an idea may not always have been used as a tool for domination, oppression and annihilation, in the main, in the hands of those in power, it has, and its impact has been profound. As an African Caribbean woman currently living on former plantation land in Jamaica, the legacy of being racialised Black permeates every single aspect of our daily existence. For us it is not a matter of theory.

The racialisation project in practice, can be traced back to the 1400s and even earlier, there is no consensus about the date, and admittedly as a process it will have existed in different forms before the term to describe it was even coined:

> As noted by Barot and Bird (2001), the term 'Racialisation' has a history going back to the end of the nineteenth century and has since engendered a diversity of understandings. These range from Fanon's interpretation of it as an equivalent of dehumanisation through Banton's suggestion that it describe Europeans' response to their encounter with people from the

developing world from the fifteenth century onwards. (Fanon, 1967; Banton, 1977)

However defined, and whenever racialisation originated it has been an ongoing catastrophic project visited in differential ways on the majority across the globe. The global minority have been the main perpetrators as part of an unequal power relationship, a myth of superiority based on skin colour and a notion of white supremacy maintained through aggressive global political, economic and cultural systems. The shared coordinates between colonisation, capitalism and racialisation are clear and expertly established in the scholarship (Eric Williams, 1964; Walter Rodney, 1972; CLR James, 1989). Later I make the connection between pseudo-science, eugenics and capitalism including drawing attention to how the work of well-known eugenicists such as Charles Darwin, Francis Galton, Margaret Sanger, Charles Davenport, Alexander Graham Bell, John Harvey Kellogg, Richard Hernstein and Charles Murray would have been synthesised into the white norm of logic, science, knowledge and modernity. Exploitation for economic gain may at one level be unethical, as Walter Rodney describes, 'when the terms of trade are set by one country in a manner entirely advantageous to itself, then the trade is usually detrimental to the trading partner'. But it takes on a whole other level of meaning when

[t]he whole import-export relationship between Africa and its trading partners is one of unequal exchange and of exploitation... When citizens of Europe own the land and the mines of Africa, this is the most direct way of sucking the African continent (dry). Under colonialism the ownership was complete and backed by military domination. (Walter Rodney, 1988, p. 22)

It is the dehumanising consequences of the racialisation process that create the wretched of the earth. I concur with Fanon's theory therefore that,

in the binary world of European thought, the development of which ran contemporaneously with colonisation, Blackness came to embody bad and Whiteness good. This process of psychological (as well as material and social) domination creates categories 'coloniser' and 'colonised', and people who are identified (and come to identify themselves) as 'black' and 'white'. As part of this relational process, he argues, the European created the' 'negro' as a category of degraded humanity: a weak, irrational barbarian, incapable of self-government. For Fanon, this psychological process, in the context of physical domination and oppression, was tantamount to dehumanising the oppressed. His understanding of racialisation was that it comprised the effects of a process instigated to relieve Europeans of guilt and to make the colonised responsible for their own oppression, because in this world view, they are too weak to rule themselves. To be racialised was thus to have been dehumanised as part of the colonial process. (Fanon, 1963)

In 2003, part of the decolonisation of the leadership development process that we were engaged in was to have Black and Asian teachers embrace their global identities and to stop collectively identifying themselves as, 'ethnic-minorities'. (Portelli & Campbell-Stephens, 2009). Apart from being an inaccurate collective term, the semantics was the least of it. A minoritised mindest was giving away the potential power that they had as part of the Global Majority. From a Pan-African perspective, self-determination was a given, continuing to use the language of the oppressor to minoritise oneself was oppositional to operating with a decolonised mindset where one named oneself. Whiteness does not operate in the interest of the majority, so why would the majority not elect to operate in its own interest? It can and has been argued that dehumanising through colonialism was in order to justify the economic exploitation, but it was taken to such extraordinary, debased lengths with African people through the transatlantic enslavement period that one has to ask was that level of depravity driven by something other than just economic gain? What role has Negritude to play in this narrative and what are we not seeing, naming, understanding, or daring to even conceive of, let alone say?

So, whether racialisation was initially intentional hundreds of years ago or not is academic, given that the overwhelming evidence of its impact over a period of 400 years has been and remains devastating. Some would argue that the level of depravity has taken its toll on all, including the oppressors, moving humanity in its entirety further away from the best version of itself. Like the mythical African Sankofa bird, in order to begin the decolonisation process, I must go back and find some of that which was lost, connect old narratives and create new ones. I have chosen where to begin.

## Before Racialisation: The Aksumite Empire (100–960 CE)

To understand the full story and what has been erased and forgotten is to appreciate that the racialisation project is not the beginning of that story, for that you have to go back centuries. There have been African civilisations that go back millennia; it has been 200,000 years since the African ancestors for all humans alive today first walked the planet.

For the purposes of this chapter, I will focus on just two African civilisations, the first, the Aksumite Empire (c. 100–960 CE), also known as the Kingdom of Aksum (or Axum), which is one of the oldest. The kingdom spread across areas that we know today as Ethiopia, Eritrea, Djibouti, Egypt, Saudi Arabia, Somalia, South Sudan, Sudan and Yemen. (Cartwright, 2019, Henze, 2000)

The Kingdom of Aksum was a major naval and trading power from the first to the seventh centuries CE. Its prosperity was due in part to its rich agricultural lands, where wheat, barley, millet and teff (a high yield grain) had been grown at least as early as the first millennium BCE with significant success due to the then dependable summer monsoon rains. Cattle herding in the Aksumite Empire dates back to the second millennium BCE.

The Aksumites were key players in the commercial trading routes which existed between the Romans and ancient India and were considered one of the four great powers of their time alongside China, Rome, and Persia. Aksum, also the name of the capital city, embraced the Orthodox tradition of Christianity in the fourth century (c. 340–356 CE). Once they converted to Christianity, they created the foundations for Ethiopia's Orthodox Church. Prior to that, the people of Axum practised an indigenous polytheistic religion, at least it was described as such by those who would write about it later. My question is whether it was the different attributes of God that these ancient religions recognised and symbolised rather than the worship of different Gods? Just to put things in context, Arabia the homeland of Arab Bedouins and the Arabian language would most probably have formed part of the Aksumite Empire. Arabia the historic birthplace of Islam and the Arab-Islamic culture which originated in the towns of Mecca and Medina did so at the beginning of the seventh century, when the Kingdom of Aksumite would have already been in existence for 600 years.

The Aksumites developed one of the continents' first indigenous scripts Ge'ez, and had its own coinage. As a civilisation, it had a profound impact upon the people of Egypt, southern Arabia, Europe and Asia, all the peoples of which visited. The kingdom went into decline from the seventh century due in part to Arab competition, but it did rise again and form the great Kingdom of Abyssinia in the thirteenth century CE which lasted until the twentieth century. The decline of this empire may have been due to a number of factors, among them, climate changes and the Islamic Empire gaining greater control of the Red Sea and most of the Nile and therefore increasing its reach and power economically in the seventh and eighth centuries.

There are several reasons for selecting the Aksumite Empire as one worthy of study as it presents an extremely powerful counter-narrative to the one usually portrayed by the West about Africa, especially when you link its history to current-day Ethiopia and the Western world.

Consider the following:

- The Aksum Empire was one of the oldest, longest and most influential empires in the world. Its influence over civilisations such as Egypt is important, given the prominence that Egypt has been given as an ancient civilisation from the continent of Africa. China, Rome, Persia and Egypt learned much from Aksum.
- Ethiopia is one of only two African countries, the other being Liberia that was never formally colonised. This is highly significant as regards the way that it is approached by the West and the rest of the world.
- The Kingdom of Aksum had its own writing system dating back to at least the second century. Yet the Sumerian language that has its roots in Iran is attested to be the oldest written language developed during the third millennium.
- Amharic is the 'working language' of the federal government; together with Oromo, it is one of the two most widely spoken languages in the country. Ethiopians are ethnically diverse, with the most important differences on the basis of linguistic categorisation. Ethiopia is a mosaic of about hundred languages that can be classified into four groups. The vast majority of languages belong to the <u>Semitic</u>, <u>Cushitic</u> or <u>Omotic</u> groups, all part of the <u>Afro-Asiatic language family</u>. A small number of languages belong to a fourth group, <u>Nilotic</u>, which is part of the <u>Nilo-Saharan language family</u>.
- The Kingdom of Aksum was a major naval and trading power, from the first to the seventh century CE, exporting ivory, gold and emeralds, and importing silks and spices—an example of mutually beneficial trade between nation states without exploitation. Ethiopia

today has a large domestic market of over 100 million people, making it the second most populous country in Africa after Nigeria. Over the last decade, Ethiopia is one of the fastest-growing economies in the world, with an average annual growth rate of 14 per cent. Ethiopia today exports coffee (28.7 per cent), oilseeds (14.5 per cent), chat (11.4 per cent), pulses (10.2 per cent), cut flowers (9.6 per cent), leather and leather products (4.4 per cent) and gold (1 per cent). Leading destinations for exports are Asia, Europe and the rest of the African continent.

- The kingdom of Aksum's wealth was in part due to rich agricultural lands, used for growing grain and cattle rearing. This suggests sophisticated irrigation systems being in place. The main exports of Aksum were agricultural products. Agriculture remains the mainstay of the Ethiopian economy today, constituting over 50 per cent of the gross domestic product (GDP), and enjoys government prioritisation and investment in supporting smallholder agriculture, eighty-five per cent of the country's labour force. Ethiopia can feed itself, through small-scale farmers who practise rain-fed mixed farming, employing traditional technology; these farmers are responsible for more than ninety per cent of the total agricultural output. The Grand Renaissance Dam in Ethiopia is the largest on the African continent and when fully completed it will be the seventh largest in the world.

- The Kingdom of Aksum practised religions before Christianity but is important in terms of Christianity for a number of reasons. The kingdom established the Ethiopian Orthodox Church and provides a beautiful example of indigenisation (Shena 1988). Its deep rootage in the lives of the people is evidenced by the way in which the church has been preserved since the fourth century in spite of repeated threats from enemies within and outside of Ethiopia. The church has Christianised important aspects of Old Testament and Hebrew culture as well as certain remnants of primal religion. Critically, it adapted beliefs and symbols which reflected and reinforced African traditions, and either absorbed or transfigured that which suited its purposes. The Ethiopian church is an indigenous church, not an indigenised one. The Abyssinian Baptist Church, in Harlem, New York, which it has been my pleasure to visit on several occasions over the years, is the first African American Baptist Church in New York. It can trace its 200-year radical theological roots right back to this ancient civilisation and church.

One of the impacts of the racialisation project has been to erase any acknowledgement and memory of the kind of history and current global influence that I have just outlined in relation to the Aksumite Empire and present-day Ethiopia. Africa's role in the world, her influence on other civilisations, the indigenous ancient knowledge that we can learn from her, have all but been swept away, stolen, hidden and misappropriated, much like her natural wealth. In order to decolonise our thinking as African people we need to be able to look back to our past, millennia before slavery, link our history to current-day contexts, ours and others; write narratives from our perspectives and live forward into a whole range of limitless possibilities, buried in our past. Instead, in the case of the continent of Africa we are more used to either one deficit narrative that begins three quarters of the way through the story, constructed by others or a kind of schizophrenic 'remembering' but more often than not 'forgetting', and always through the white lens, which brings me to my second African empire.

## THE BENIN EMPIRE (1180–1897 CE)

European museums are crammed full of artefacts looted from former empires that were never supposed to have existed if certain narratives are to be believed. The Benin Empire in Nigeria (c. 1180 CE–1897 CE) is one such example. It was considered to be one of the oldest and most developed states in West Africa until its annexation and destruction by the British Empire. The Benin Empire had a strong trading relationship with the Portuguese in the sixteenth century and later in the sixteenth and seventeenth centuries with the British starting in 1553; until in the case of the British, Benin suspected them of making 'controlling advancements'. Famous artisans created works of art from ivory, bronze, brass, wood and iron. The Benins traded palm oil, pepper and ivory. The narratives up until this point of the Dutch, British and Portuguese explorers about Benin were one of 'beauty, wealth and sophistication':

'The social structure was complex and sophisticated, and the territory well developed with the Oba residing in well-fortified beautifully designed palace', the captain of a Portuguese ship, Lourenco Pinto, (also) observed that:
 'Great Benin, where the King resides, is larger than Lisbon, all the streets run straight and as far as the eyes can see. The houses are large, especially that of the king which is richly decorated and has fine columns. The city is

wealthy and industrious. It is so well governed that theft is unknown and the people live in such security that they have no door to their houses'.

Yet, in February 1897, the City of Benin was burnt to the ground and the Oba's palace destroyed and looted of its magnificent and valuable bronze and ivory sculptures by the British. The sacking of Benin was described by Dan Hicks (2020) as an attack on human life, on culture, on belief, on art, and on sovereignty.

In addition, he states,

> The British atrocity at Benin City was a crime against humanity that mapped directly onto the three principal elements of the 1899 Hague Convention: the indiscriminate attack on human life in which tens of thousands died; the purposeful and proactive destruction of an ancient cultural, religious and royal site; and the looting of sacred artworks. The Hague Convention banned the bombardment of 'undefended settlements, villages or towns', while also banning bullets, like the' 'soft-point' .303 full metal jackets, that were designed to expand when they hit humans, along with any other 'arms, projectiles, or material of a nature to cause superfluous injury. (Hicks, 2020)

The Convention went on in various articles to prohibit destruction of 'edifices devoted to religion, art, and science' as well as the destruction or seizure of property. In addition, the Convention repeatedly stated that 'the pillage of a town or place, even when taken by assault is prohibited' (Article 28). And under Article 46, 'private property cannot be confiscated' and pillage is formally prohibited in Article 47. By the time the Convention came into effect, on 4 September 1900, the Royal Niger Company had been sold to the British Crown.

At the heart of this barbarity is the drafting of a new narrative by the British and other Europeans in Africa. In the case of the utter destruction and ransacking of Benin and the British, the details were left deliberately vague as regards the numbers of men, women and children massacred, but they did celebrate the ingenuity of their 'soft-point' bullets with their tips removed so that they could expand on impact with human flesh causing maximum suffering, pain and carnage. Why such psychopathic depravity on the part of the British towards African, men, women and children? European museums have played their role as a conduit for spreading the single false narrative of the African continent, that has served to racialise, dehumanise and subjugate the African, while normalising crimes against humanity, when that humanity is African.

Since the modern age the museum has been a powerful device of separation. The exhibiting of subjugated or humiliated humanities has always adhered to certain elementary rules of injury and violation. These humanities have never had the right in the museum to the same treatment, status or dignity as the conquering humanities. They have always been subjected to other rules of classification and other logics of presentation.

By 1897 the violent sacking by British troops of the City of Benin a pivotal moment in the formation of Nigeria as a British colony, changed the narrative for modern-day Nigeria completely. Objects looted from the City of Benin are on display in an estimated 161 museums and galleries in Europe and North America, while at the same time the myth of Africa as the dark continent was gathering pace, not least in the text of Joseph Conrad's short story Heart of Darkness, that first appeared in 1899, and was published in 1902.

The deliberate lie that has been projected on Africa by the white man is that of calling Africa the dark continent, due, so the rationale goes, to the European not knowing much about the continent until the nineteenth century. This we know to be a lie. Europeans knew a great deal about Africa over many centuries for at least 2000 years. It was a deliberate, intentional strategy driven by imperial impulses to racialise, demonise, humiliate, colonise, destroy and dehumanise through one false narrative the continent of Africa and its people.

My reason for selecting the Benin empire is that Nigeria is currently the most populous country in Africa and is destined to be the most populous and youthful Black Country in the world. Part of the resetting that is taking place is through institutions like the British Museum coming to terms with its colonial past, as it quietly returns at least some of the artefacts that it stole and murdered for in the name of empire. Dan Hicks is uncompromising as he writes about his book titled *The Brutish Museums*:

> And so, this is a book about sovereignty and violence, about how museums were co-opted into the nascent project of protofacism through the looting of African sovereignty, and about how museums can resist that racist legacy today. It is at the same time a kind of defense of the importance of anthropology museums, as places that decentre European culture, worldviews, and prejudices—but only if such museums transform themselves by facing up to the enduring presence of empire, including through acts of cultural restitu-

tion and reparations, and for the transformation of a central part of the purpose of these spaces into sites of conscience. It is therefore a book about a wider British reckoning with the brutishness of our Victorian colonial history, to which museums represent a unique index, and important spaces in which to make those pasts visible. The Pitt Rivers Museum is not a national museum, but it is a brutish museum. Along with other anthropology museums, it allowed itself to become a vehicle for a militarist vision of white supremacy through the display of the loot of so-called 'small wars' in Africa. The purpose of this book is to change the course of these brutish museums, to redefine them as public spaces, sites of conscience, in which to face up to the ultraviolence of Britain's colonial past in Africa, and its enduring nature, and in which to begin practical steps towards African cultural restitution. (Hicks, 2020)

## WHITENESS, EUROCENTRISM, WHITE SUPREMACY AND OTHER DELUSIONS

In a global context where power has historically been structured by racialisation, whiteness and white supremacy are baked into the white psyche as normal and maintained in part through hatred, and sometimes fear of Black people. Normative Whiteness has now taken on a whole new meaning of significance; whiteness is now in 2021 a central driver for cultural and political affairs. Ta-Nehisi Coates described whiteness as 'an existential danger to the country and the world'. Like race, whiteness is a social construct, dependent on its relationship to Blackness, which has been one of subjugation, deemed necessary for whiteness to have any meaning and power:

> The discovery of personal Whiteness took place during the second half of the seventeenth century, on the peripheries of the still-young British empire. What's more, historians such as Oscar and Mary Handlin, Edmund Morgan and Edward Rugemer have largely confirmed DuBois's suspicion that while xenophobia appears to be fairly universal among all human groupings including Black and Brown people, the invention of a white racial identity was motivated from the start by a need to justify the enslavement of Africans and their reduction to property. The relationality between White and Black then took on new meaning. In the words of Eric Williams, a historian 'slavery was not born of racism: rather, racism was the consequence of slavery'. (Baird, 2021)

Imperialism therefore while global to the Western businessmen in the nineteenth century, was different when it came to what some described as 'the imperialist hunger for Africa' compared to other parts of the world. Having dehumanised Africans for at least 200 years through enslavement on Caribbean and American plantations, imperialism where Africans and Europeans were concerned was quite different. Most empire-building begins with the recognition of trading and commercial benefits that could be accrued, and up to a point, this was the case between Europeans and Africans before the enslavement period, see the Aksumite and Benin empires as examples.

After enslavement, in Africa's case, from then on, the continent as a whole was being annexed to fulfil three purposes: the white man's spirit of adventure, provide the context in which to support good work of 'civilising the native', and, tellingly stamp out the trading power of enslaved African people. Writers such as H. Ryder Haggard, Joseph Conrad and Rudyard Kipling fed into the romantic depiction of a place that required saving by strong men of adventure:

> An explicit duality was set up for these adventurers: dark versus light and Africa versus West. The idea of a hostile Nature and a disease-ridden environment as tinged with evil was perpetrated by fictional accounts by Joseph Conrad (1899) and authors such as W. Somerset Maugham. (Thompsell, 2020)

In The Heart of Darkness (1899), Conrad depicted Africa as an erotically and psychologically powerful place of darkness, one that could only be cured by a direct application of Christianity and, of course, capitalism. Geographer Lucy Jarosz describes this stated and unstated belief clearly: Africa was seen as

> a primeval, bestial, reptilian, or female entity to be tamed, enlightened, guided, opened, and pierced by white European males through western science, Christianity, civilisation, commerce, and colonialism. (Jarosz, 1992)

By the 1870s and 1880s, European traders, officials and adventurers were going to Africa to seek their fame and fortune, the then recent developments in weaponry gave these men significant power in Africa. When they abused that power, especially in places like the Congo, Europeans blamed the Dark Continent, rather than themselves. 'Africa, they said, was what supposedly brought out the savagery in man.'

The myths continue today. Over the years, endless reasons have been proffered as to why Africa was labelled 'the Dark Continent'. People who have not done the research think it is a racist phrase but cannot say why, and so the common belief has developed in recent times that the phrase just referred to Europe's lack of knowledge about Africa, making the phrase 'Dark Continent' seem in 2021 outdated, but otherwise benign. Those who have done the research know differently. Race does lie at the heart of this myth, but it is not about skin colour. The myth of the Dark Continent refers to the savagery that Europeans said was endemic to Africa, which was actually the savagery inflicted by Europeans on Africa, erasing centuries of pre-colonial history, contact and travel across Africa. In the process of dehumanising Africans, Europeans reduced themselves to subhumans.

As part of the racialisation process there have been historical episodes, narratives created by white people, that have exemplified and reinforced 'whiteness' sometimes through religion as dominant, superior and placing white people at the top of the hierarchy of human value; these historical episodes, several operating concurrently, are summarily chronicled below, and include:

The Crusades 1095, where white Christian Europeans superiority was the argument used for conquests in Asia.

The Spanish Inquisition (1478–1834), which was the persecution of Jews and Muslims and the beginning of the racialisation of Islam.

### Voyages of Columbus to the New World (3 August 1492–1504)

Columbus made four transatlantic voyages: 1492–1493, 1493–1496, 1498–1500 and 1502–1504. He travelled primarily to the Caribbean, including the Bahamas, Cuba, Santo Domingo and Jamaica, and in his latter two voyages travelled to the coasts of eastern Central America and northern South America. Columbus's arrival was followed by the genocidal destruction of the indigenous peoples of Bahamas, Cuba Santa Domingo and Jamaica before landing on the coasts of Central America and Southern America.

## Transatlantic European 'Slave-Traders': Fifteenth to Nineteenth Century

By the 1480s, the Portuguese were already transporting Africans for use as slaves on the sugar plantations in the Madeira and Cape Verde islands. The Spanish took Africans to the Caribbean where they were enslaved after 1502, but Portuguese merchants continued to dominate the transatlantic slave trade for another century and a half, operating from their bases in the Congo-Angola area along the west coast of Africa. In the 1600s the Dutch became the foremost slave-traders, and in the following century English and French merchants controlled about half of the transatlantic slave trade, taking a large percentage of their human cargo from the region of West Africa.

## Barbados Plantation and the 1661 Slave Codes: White Race 'Invented' and Established in Law

Barbados was the first place to create a unique racialised demography described in law, where whiteness indicated entitlement and white people accrued benefits as a result of being white. In 1661 Walrond created two comprehensive pieces of legislation 'An act for the good governing of Servants, and ordaining the Rights between Masters and Servants' and 'An act for the better ordering and governing of Negroes'—that set the tone for the creation of a society stratified by race and colour. By law, white-skinned people could enjoy power, freedom and wealth at the expense of a Black population subjugated by brute force. The Barbados slave codes were designed to oppress by a systematic negation of the most basic human rights of Black people. The servants originally referred to were indentured white servants, largely of Irish extraction.

## The Slave Codes in Jamaica: 1664

In 1664, Thomas Modyford left Barbados for Jamaica. He was to be its new governor. He took with him papers including the Slave Codes. He was accompanied by 800 planters. The following five years saw the import of 5000 Africans to Jamaica where previously there had been less than 600 enslaved Africans who were being imported to work on Jamaican plantations, where they were subject to a vicious regime of labour and severe punishments. Modyford presided over the debauched Jamaican capital

Port Royal, home to pirates like Henry Morgan. The Slave Codes normalised this brutality and they were used on enslaved Africans, with Jamaica being the breaking ground, before the practice was spread across the Caribbean and in North America for the next 200 years.

### Colonial Virginia: 1660–1690

Slave codes in Virginia were amended to suit local conditions, including using the notion of whiteness in law to exclude. Slaves who ran away twice were to be gelded and the women lost an ear. Gelding as a punishment had no precedent in English law, and neither Jamaica nor Barbados had legislated for it. So, another level of dehumanising Black men literally treating them as beasts with a procedure that would have normally be reserved for cattle was introduced in Virginia. Between 1660 and 1690, leaders of the Virginia colony began to pass laws and establish practices that provided or sanctioned differential treatment for freed servants whose origins were in Europe. This was similar to what happened in Barbados and Jamaica. African Americans and Africans, mulattoes, and American Indians, regardless of their cultural similarities or differences, were forced into categories separate from whites. Historical records also show that the Virginia Assembly went to great extremes not only to purposely separate Europeans from Indians and Africans, but to promote contempt on the part of whites, against Black people.

### Elizabeth Key (Kaye): 1655

In 1655, a mulatto (bi-racial) woman named Elizabeth Key (or Kaye) sued for her freedom and that of her son, John. Her suit for freedom rested on several factors. First, she was the daughter of Thomas Key, an English planter and an enslaved woman. English common law dictated that a child inherited the status of its father. Second Elizabeth's father had arranged an indenture under which she would be freed at the age of fifteen, but that contract had been violated. Finally, Elizabeth had been baptised in the Church of England and was a practising Christian. One decision allowed Elizabeth her freedom on account of her father's freedom, but another denied her liberty because of her mother's enslaved status. Eventually, the case rose to the Virginia General Assembly, which resolved 'that by the Common Law the Child of a Woman slave begot by a freeman ought to be free'. 'They considered the value of her Christian faith and determined that her indenture demanded that she be treated' 'more Respectfully than a Common servant or slave'. After determining the freedom of Elizabeth and her son, the General Assembly returned the case to the lower courts, where they freed Elizabeth.

Prior to the court cases, Elizabeth Kay and William Greensted had a son, John. They were legally married in July 1656 after the court freed Elizabeth and John, and William completed his own indenture. However, by 1662, Virginia legislators resolved that the condition of the mother determined the status of the child, this was the opposite to what had previously been the practices of English common law—effectively making slavery a hereditary status, when the child was born to a Black woman.

### Race, Whiteness and Citizenship: In the USA, 1790

Penned by the very first US Congress, the first US Naturalisation Act of 1790, excluded everyone who was not white:

> In 1790 the young republic's first Congress wrote whiteness into the legal structures of US citizenship by stipulating that only 'free white persons' could immigrate and become naturalized citizens. This according to Matthew Frye Jacobson was perhaps the 'most portentous law in US history,' both for the political world it created and for what it might tell us about the operations of 'race' in our national life. (Frye-Jacobson, 2014)

*The Scramble for Africa, also called the Partition of Africa, Conquest of Africa, or the Rape of Africa*, was the invasion, occupation, division, and colonisation of most of Africa by seven Western European powers during a short period known to historians as the New Imperialism between 1881 and 1914. The ten per cent of Africa that was under formal European control in 1870 increased to almost ninety per cent of the continent by 1914, with only Ethiopia (Abyssinia) and Liberia remaining independent and uncolonised. The Berlin Conference of 1884, which regulated European colonisation and trade in Africa, is usually referred to as the starting point of the Scramble for Africa.

### Jewish Holocaust (1941–1945) During World War II

The systematic state-sponsored persecution and mass murder of millions of European Jews, as well as millions of others, including Romani people, the intellectually disabled, dissidents and homosexuals by the German Nazi regime between 1933 and 1945.

## RACE SCIENCE

Race and racism are not new issues and they continue to be polarising and incendiary. There is agreement that neither race nor ethnicity is detectable in the human genome; while there are population groups that share a high amount of genetic inheritance such as physical characteristics like hair texture and colour of skin, individuals often share more genes with 'other races' than they do with members of 'their own race'. Therefore 'race' cannot be definitively defined biologically, but we can cluster groups into rough geographic regions, often initially at least on physical and other genetically inherited characteristics. It is accepted that race is a social construct, that it is problematic and tricky, race science even more so, but racism is real and you can still ask Google, 'What are the three human races?' and receive an answer, such is the ambivalence.

One can trace the roots of racism, back to The Crusades and race science to slavery and colonialism. So, while the science may be deemed as discredited in some academic circles, not by any means all, the thinking that formed the basis of race science continues to influence mainstream policy, practice and discourse and that is dangerous because of its populist appeal to a minority, contemptuous of the majority, and it promotes whiteness as the norm at the top of the hierarchy (Herrnstein & Murray, 1996). Race impacts lives profoundly.

In 1969 when Arthur Jensen, an American psychologist claimed that IQ was eighty per cent a product of our genes rather than our environments, and that the differences between Black and white IQs were largely rooted in genetics, this was accepted fact. This thinking informs to this day all kinds of social policy, including education systems, policies and practices. Standardised Assessment Tests (SATS) used in our schools, for example, come from these geneticist roots.

In apartheid South Africa, the idea that each race had its own character, personality traits and intellectual potential was part of the justification for the system of white rule. The subject of race and IQ was similarly politicised in the USA, where Jensen's paper was used to oppose welfare schemes, such as the Head Start programme, 'which were designed to lift children out of poverty' (Gavin Evans, 2018). The same thing happened in England 2013 when Dominic Cummings, a then Government Adviser, wrote his 250-page paper entitled 'Genetics Outweighs Teaching', essentially attacking fear of elitism and bemoaning the waste of billions of pounds on programmes like Sure Start in the UK, which was similar to Head Start in the USA. While the rebuttal of Head Start met with stiff resistance in the USA, the response to the equivalent programmes being shelved in the UK were much more muted.

My awakening to the pervasiveness of race science thinking and the positioning of whiteness to exclude came early in my career as a teacher. British schools were already operating under the guise of race science in the 1960s, when children of West Indian heritage were first entering the education system in numbers due to large-scale migration from the then West Indies in the 1950s of their parents. A recent (2021) TV documentary exposed the apartheid system that was operating in Britain, including the existence of educationally subnormal schools to which the majority of Caribbean heritage children were sent in the 1960s and 1970s. As a student teacher in the late 1970s/early 1980s we were highly aware of how the structurally racist system worked and many of us joined Pan-African organisations who among other initiatives ran African Caribbean Saturday Schools in which we taught alongside our full-time teaching job in mainstream schools. These schools could be found in several major cities in England, including London, Birmingham, Nottingham, Bristol, Leeds and Liverpool.

The seminal work 'How the West Indian Child is made Educationally Subnormal in the British Education System' by Bernard Coard was as much part of my socialisation as a young teacher within Pan-African organisations, as was much later when I was an Ofsted Inspector in 1994 *The Bell Curve* by Richard Herrnstein and Charles Murray. The book argued that poor people, and particularly poor Black people, were inherently less intelligent than white or Asian people. And in 2021, *The Bell Curve*, described by the Scientific American (2017) as 'the flagship modern work reporting on racial differences in IQ', is making a resurgence in popularity. This is extremely worrying, (a) because it condones prejudgment and (b) endorses prejudice based on race; and (c) it promotes white supremacy while perpetrating an epistemology of ignorance (Sullivan & Tuana, 2007), challenging at an individual level, catastrophic at the public policy level.

## Conclusion

> in order to fully acknowledge the importance of differences, especially in the global era, we first have to critically confront the histories of domination and violation within which they are constituted. (De Lissovoy, 2010)

Importantly this historical chapter took some time to write. The intention was to provide an overview of the chronology of racialisation and the development of whiteness. But the way to understand this chapter is not to see the set of events in a linear line from the first century to the present but to borrow an analogy from Matthew Frye Jacobson to see history more like geological layers, starting with the present at the top with layers going down, thereby making history ever present in the soil on which we build.

The detail was necessary about the Aksumite and Benin empires to expose the contradictions in white narratives about Africa, such as they have something worth stealing, murdering and lying about, for example, the Benin bronzes, as addressed in 'The Brutish Museums'—Dan Hicks (2020), or, 'there is nothing to see here' as the narrative perpetuated through stories such as Joseph Conrad's, 'Heart of Darkness'. Both are lies. Civilisations existed in Africa long before the Europeans arrived:

> The moment that the topic of the pre-European African past is raised, many individuals are concerned for various reasons to know about the existence of African 'civilizations.' Mainly, this stems from a desire to make comparisons with European 'civilizations.' This is not the context in which to evaluate the so-called civilizations of Europe. It is enough to note the behaviour of European capitalists from the epoch of slavery through colonialism, fascism, and genocidal wars in Asia and Africa. Such barbarism causes suspicion to attach to the use of the word 'civilisation'. (Rodney, 1972)

The racial dynamics and divisions that the process of racialisation precipitated, and in other cases exacerbated, but certainly at all levels exploited, between and within different groups and the hierarchies created based on colour, are an essential part of the narrative ripe for deconstruction. Whiteness continues to orient people in different ways, but a reckoning with the myth of white solidarity and superiority now beckons as the global masses begin to push back on a number of fronts critical to self-determination, social justice and humankind's survival, literally as if their lives depended on it, because it does.

The erasure of histories spread over millennia is one of the most cata-strophic forms of genocide to have ever been visited on humankind, which is why so much time was devoted to the reconstruction of our knowledge about the Aksumite Empire. The chapter contends that one of the deepest and profound injuries has been the psychological trauma visited upon gen-erations of Africans, and most importantly their descendants, including those in the Diaspora, who form an important part of the Global Majority, often without memory, being unconscious of their central contribution to global history and the present modern-day society.

The global minority continue through to the present day to diminish the importance and contribution of the continent of Africa to the world. Her people have influenced civilisations, with knowledge, culture, science and art. In addition, neo-colonialists while orchestrating as well as weav-ing narratives of African corruption, famine and war, continue through their fiscal policies, and political destabilisation, in former African colonies to monopolise real estate and resources, in the interests of the former colonisers. The continent of Africa is larger than Europe, China, India and the USA combined. Rich in oil and natural resources, the continent holds a strategic position. It is the world's fastest-growing regions for foreign direct investment, and it has approximately thirty per cent of the earth's remaining mineral resources. It has vast oil and natural gas deposits; the Sahara holds the most strategic nuclear ore; and resources such as coltan essential for the fourth industrial technological revolution, gold and cop-per, among many other precious metals, are abundant across the conti-nent. The African continent has the youngest demographic on the planet. But Africa's development is still being arrested by the very countries that rely on it for their wealth and status.

That form of arrested development or neo-colonialism is predicated on African countries continuing to pay heavily for their 'independence' from former colonisers, though tax, debt and currency tied to, for example, the French franc (and the continued wealth building of countries like France)—or in the case of smaller countries like Jamaica, having under-development cemented into fiscal policy for generations by institutions such as the International Monetary Fund (IMF), requiring recurrent devaluation of the Jamaican dollar to punish the former Prime Minister Michael Manley for not agreeing to their stringent and pernicious mone-tary regulations. Multinational corporations have taken over from Western and European industrialised countries in plundering real estate, and the natural resources from the continent and across the global south on which they have relied over centuries and still do, to build the wealth and power of the developed world, while reducing the developing world largely through globalisation and neo-colonial fiscal policies to rubble and the veritable 'shithole countries' as described by Trump.

It is the developed world that is dependent on Africa, not the other way around, yet the dominant narratives, largely perpetrated through the Western media, international aid agencies and the International Monetary Fund (IMF), tell a very different story. Sticking with the French example, the CFA Franc, brought into use in 1945, is tied to the Euro, and requires countries that were former French colonies to channel at least fifty per cent of their foreign reserves through French banks, to which countries only have access to fifteen per cent of their money per year. It is estimated that approximately the equivalent of 500 billion Euros a year of African countries' revenues are in the French treasury, filtered back to the countries of origin, through aid. These systems rely on maintaining an unhealthy co-dependency in which sovereign states remain subordinated to their colonial masters.

The alternative narrative intended to justify the continued minoritisation and subordination is one based on a lie, its origins located in depicting the African as a subhuman savage, then slave, then Black, what is consistent is that the African is always at the bottom of the hierarchy. In various contexts and at different times throughout history, the African has been dehumanised, commoditised and colonised by the non-African. In answering the questions how did whiteness and the white man, the minority, become, the superior human, the default human? The historical process of racialisation and the development of whiteness cannot be disaggregated from imperialism, colonialism and capitalism.

In the coming chapters we step outside of the binary of Black and white, European and African encounters to examine how racialisation works in other contexts, but it was important to go into the detail in this chapter examining the racialisation of Africans by Europeans, especially for the dehumanisation piece and to understand the process at its most destructive, with generational consequences deliberately entrenched:

Maldonado-Torres (2008) calls this a 'master morality' premised on an absolute refusal to engage the colonized person as ethical being; for Mills (1997), this is the discursive norming of non-white bodies as sub-human. This systematic blindness to the actual violence of conquest, and to the fact of philosophy's historical complicity in the projects of material, epistemological, and spiritual subjugation, results in a crucial gap or failure in the dominant discourses of ethics and politics, even as they congeal into the hegemonic common senses of everyday life. (De Lissovoy, 2010)

## REFERENCES

Baird, R. P. (2021). The invention of Whiteness: The long history of a dangerous idea. *The Guardian*.

Cartwright, M. (2019, March 21). Kingdom of Axum. *World History Encyclopedia*. https://www.worldhistory.org/Kingdom_of_Axum/

Conrad, J. (1902). Heart of darkness. *Blackwood's Magazine*.

De Lissovoy, N. (2010). Decolonial pedagogy and the ethics of the global. *Discourse: Studies in the Cultural Politics of Education, 31*(3), 279–293. https://doi.org/10.1080/01596301003786886

Dei, G. (1996). Critical perspectives in antiracism: An introduction. *Canadian Review of Sociology, 33*(3), 247–267.

Evans, G. (2018). The unwelcome revival of 'race science'. *The Guardian*.

Fanon, F. (1963). *The wretched of the earth* (C. Farrington, Trans.). Grove Press.

Fanon, F. (1967). *Black skin, white masks* (L. Markmann, Trans.). Grove Press.

Frye-Jacobson, M. (2014). *Whiteness and the normative American citizen*. A talk on the US Naturalisation Act (1790).

Henze, P. B. (2000). The Aksumite Empire. In *Layers of time*. Palgrave Macmillan. https://doi.org/10.1007/978-1-137-11786-1_2

Herrnstein, R. J., & Murray, C. (1996). *The Bell curve. Intelligence and class structure in American life*. Simon and Schuster.

Hicks, D. (2020). *The Brutish museums, the Benin Bronzes, colonial violence and cultural restitution*. Pluto Press. Kindle Edition.

James, C. L. R. (1989). *The Black Jacobins: Toussaint L'Ouverture and the San Domingo revolution*. W H Allen and Co Plc.

Jarosz, L. (1992). Constructing the dark continent: Metaphor as geographic representation of Africa. *Geografiska Annaler. Series B, Human Geography, 74*(2), 105–115. Taylor & Francis, Ltd.

Kempf, H., & Moizeau, F. (2009). Inequality, growth and the dynamics of social segmentation. *Journal of Public Economic Theory, 11*(4), 529–564. Wiley Periodicals, Inc.

Portelli, J., & Campbell-Stephens, R. (2009). *Leading for equity: The investing in diversity approach*. EdPhil Books.

Rodney, W. (1972). *How Europe underdeveloped Africa*. Bogle-L Ouverture Publications.

Selvarajah, S., Deivanayagam, T. A., Lasco, G., et al. (2020). Categorisation and minoritisation. *BMJ Global Health, 5*, e004508. https://doi.org/10.1136/bmjgh-2020-004508

Sullivan, S., & Tuana, N. (2007). *Race and epistemologies of ignorance*. State University of New York Press.

Thompsell, A. (2020, August 29). Why was Africa called the dark continent? *ThoughtCo*, thoughtco.com/why-africa-called-the-dark-continent-43310

Williams, E. (1964). *Capitalism and slavery*. Andre Deutsch.

# CHAPTER 3

# Disrupting Narratives: Language Power and Self-determination

**Abstract** This chapter focuses on how the language of the coloniser is weaponised to eradicate any authentic expression of the colonised, to subjugate, dominate, erase or delegitimise their culture, knowledge and collective memory. The chapter examines how the erasure of language is a form of violence, colonialism and dehumanisation. It reflects on how the sidelining of languages other than English upholds epistemic systems such as modernity and development. In addition, it explores power hierarchies. Key to this is illuminating how the racialised hierarchy of language is used as a colonial process to transmit values, ideas and narratives represented as universal or global ideals while delegitimising indigenous knowledge. The conceptualisation of Investing in Diversity as a decolonising process in leadership preparation for school leaders began with disrupting the narratives about Black and Minority Ethnic (BAME) leadership and underrepresentation in London schools. The chapter explores how people of the Global Majority can utilise their agency in narrative remembering, collating, shaping and sharing to disrupt and reimagine indigenous epistemologies from a global south perspective. Essentially, it examines how the decolonisation process must begin within the minds of the Global Majority.

**Keywords** Language • Power • Race

© The Author(s), under exclusive license to Springer Nature Switzerland AG 2021
R. M. Campbell-Stephens, *Educational Leadership and the Global Majority*, https://doi.org/10.1007/978-3-030-88282-2_3

## Language, Power, Legitimacy and Race

A fully functioning human needs language to think, solve problems, express emotions and relate to others in a coherent and cohesive way. Therefore, language is important to cultural identity and self-identity. Professor Rex Nettleford, a Jamaican scholar, termed this human experience of self-worth as the feeling of 'smaddiness', using the Jamaican vernacular. As a British-born person of Jamaican parents, I am as wedded to my form of patois as I am to the English language. Both speak directly to how I identify:

> When we speak the language of the coloniser, as Fanon (2008) states, the question is not just whose language is being spoken, but what values, ideas and cultures are being reproduced and represented as universal or global ideals. It also asks which languages have currency and which are gobbled up, disciplined and marginalised as a direct result of privileging particular languages. (Phillipson, 1992, 2001, 2008)

Through centuries of violent Western imperialism, colonialism, neo-colonialism and more recently, globalisation, the West has spread its preferred systems of capitalism, religion, education, democracy and moral values, to name but a few, through the proliferation of English as a universal language. Language is therefore a central consideration in any kind of decolonial work. Apart from the ideas, the values and the vocabulary, the very process of thinking, the tone, the attitude and the parameters of thought are dictated by the language. And when your own language has been ripped away from you and replaced by the language of the coloniser, the ambivalence you have about the capacity of that language to deliver the liberation that it was instrumental in taking away, never quite leaves you.

The benign acceptance today of English as the default language of choice is one of the ways that colonisation remains firmly in place, with its weaponry celebrated, even revered (Roche 2019). One of the counter arguments for linguistic imperialism is that the languages that the Europeans took to Asia and Africa, for example, now enable Asians and Africans to form international bonds with the rest of the world and are even necessary for internal national unity, with local languages positioned extraordinarily as oppositional and divisive.

In the Caribbean education context, Dr Patriam Smith notes the following in a presentation to Shortwood Teachers' College in Jamaica in

2021: 'The positioning of the home language as a problem in a post-colonial Caribbean is problematic.' Language serves a purpose above and beyond conveying meaning; its role in maintaining culture is essential, but seeing cultural difference as richness, rather than oppositional and divisive, is key. Dr Smith goes further: 'The non-racialised speaker using the language of power is heard as intelligent, because the language of power is at the top of the hierarchy.' This would have struck home to a Caribbean audience that values highly the capacity to speak the 'Queen's English' with even more aplomb than the English do themselves. But I wonder how they heard Dr Smith's next assertion, namely that 'language erasure and language imposition is part of the process of dehumanisation' (Smith, 2021).

I was reflecting on how Caribbean, or indeed any formally colonised people, can find a way to true independence, autonomy and self-determination in a post-colonial setting through the coloniser's language as the only vehicle. I remembered the power of listening to Nelson Mandela respond to an interview question posed at a largely white town hall meeting in 1990 in the USA. He challenged the questioner's (a white man's) right to assume that Madiba's perception of leaders that the West had deemed as enemies would be the same as the questioner's opinion of said leaders. Mandela did so eloquently in English. Later in the same presentation, he chose first to respond in his own language of Xhosa, and then translate, joking with the chair, that he 'just wanted to demonstrate that he was bilingual'. He demonstrated more than that. It took me back to the original question, the unspoken assumption that given the support that some white power structures had given to Mandela's release from prison, those Black, Arab and Cuban leaders that the West had labelled as personas non-grata would be equally labelled so by him; he disabused them of that. Mr Mandela was speaking English but he had independence of thought, different to those embodied in the language that he used to respond. In electing to respond first in Xhosa to a later question, he demonstrated how that independence of thought could be enjoyed, empowered and shared when you think and speak in your own language essentially to and for yourself and your own people. It was powerful African Narrative (You Tube 2020).

I grew up in the city that was once at the heart of the Industrial Revolution, Birmingham. At one time the city was known as the first manufacturing town in the world. Among the tools exported to Jamaica during the period of African enslavement would be the instruments of torture to prevent Africans communicating with each other.

wa Thiong'o reminds us,

> [T]he choice of language and the use to which language is put is central to a people's definition of themselves ... hence language has always been at the heart of the two contending social forces in the Africa of the twentieth century. (wa Thiong'o, 1994 [1986])

wa Thiong'o's proposition is that when the capitalists of Europe in 1884 re-carved the African continent the Berlin-drawn division under which Africa is still living was obviously economic and political, but it was also cultural. Berlin in 1884 saw the division of Africa into the different languages of the European powers. African countries as colonies and even today as neo-colonies, came to be defined and to define themselves in terms of the languages of Europe: English-speaking, French-speaking or Portuguese-speaking African countries (wa Thiong'o, 1994 [1986]).

Language is as powerful as the gun. More so: it can subjugate your mind as well as your body.

The English language undeniably has agency. Today, English is the third most spoken language in the world and tops the list of second languages About 1.8 billion people speak it. This is after for more than a century being the most widely spoken language in the world. As such, it has become the world's main communication tool, including in its former colonies. Jamaica enjoys a certain status in the Caribbean for being the largest English-speaking island, for example. English is viewed as an international language, a tool that links different societies. To illustrate a different characteristic attributed to English, it is the norm for non-native English speakers to communicate with other non-native English speakers in English. If they do not share a native language, it becomes the default. This makes English very powerful, and this power can be used for good or ill. It is the language for business, diplomacy, education, entertainment, medicine and science:

> Although many of the formally colonised populations have today gained what is usually called political independence, the cultural and linguistic decolonisation of both European and non-European cultures is hardly complete. Particularly since the second world war a struggle has been ongoing that attempts to remove the stigma from non-European cultures and languages, and questions the assumed European superiority. (Migge & Léglise, 2007)

As a woman of African Caribbean descent, I am acutely aware of the role that the English language and English language speakers have played in the subjugation of my ancestors. English has also been used as a weapon of mass destruction and dehumanisation through colonisation (Cesaire 1972). So, my relationship with the English language is one of ambivalence, especially as a former teacher of English. I am unable, for example, to trace my African ancestry back beyond great-grandparents who would have been born into enslavement in the Caribbean, punished for speaking in their own language, and given one anglicised name about which little is documented. The development of surnames in Jamaica for the enslaved came by one of two routes, both of which denoted ownership by white people and removal from the African human self. All of this occurred under the yoke of the English, with their language as a primary tool of oppression and subjugation, alongside the whip.

Until the nineteenth century the English were a major superpower and their method of colonisation included establishing schools which taught the English language and Western culture. As English becomes the global norm for large-scale business, innovation and science, indigenous languages rich in cultural heritage and history get put to one side, as they serve no function in the globalised economy. A routine examination of languages taught at GCSE in secondary school level in the UK in 2021, for example, will show that there is not one African language offered among the eighteen or so languages that can be studied.

In 2010 when visiting South Africa, I visited the Hector Pieterson Museum in Soweto. This is a museum dedicated to preserving the memory of the 1976 uprising of students in Soweto who had been protesting against the enforcement of teaching in Afrikaans and the third-rate quality of schooling that they were receiving under Bantu education. Over 350 children died that day, some as young as eight years old, shot at point-blank range by white South African police. These students understood the power of language, the erasure of identity, violently imposed and enforced by the coloniser's bullets. The museum outside which I was standing in 2010 was named after Hector Pieterson, who was one of the students shot and killed on 16 June 1976, aged 13. In 1976 I was 15 years old, and I remember hearing about the Soweto uprising, and even seeing some of it on the TV. At age 19, it was one of the key reasons that I joined the Pan-African Caribbean Self-Help Organisation's Saturday school as a volunteer teacher. There, among the many posters on the wall, was the iconic image of Hector Pieterson's limp and bloodied body being carried by a young man. Running alongside them in that black and white photo was a young female student in her school uniform, crying. As I arrived at the museum in Soweto, I was confronted by that iconic photo, larger than life, outside. It took me straight back to being a fifteen-year-old student some thirty-plus years previously, and then to the nineteen-year-old student teacher in Handsworth, Birmingham, and I started to cry. As I composed myself and entered the museum, I tried to explain to the guide, Antoinette Sithole, what the image outside meant to me. When she told me that she was Hector Pieterson's sister and the young woman in the photo, it brought me to my knees.

In the face of our history, knowing what we know, and cannot unknow, how as African educators can we be any less than we are?

## LANGUAGE OPENING AND CLOSING DOORS

While the critique has so far been of English, because of its global prominence, 'language oppression' as a form of domination has not been the sole preserve of the English. Scholars have defined language oppression as the 'enforcement of language loss by physical, mental, social and spiritual coercion'. One of many examples of language suppression and erasure today would be the Tibetans and Uyghur in the People's Republic of China:

> In 1492 Queen Isabella of Spain was presented with a plan for establishing Castilian as a tool for conquest abroad and a weapon to suppress untutored speech at home: for its author, Antonio de Nebrija, 'Language has always been the consort of empire, and forever shall remain its mate' (Illich, 1981, pp. 34–35). 'The language was to be fashioned as a standard in the domestic education system, as a means of social control, and harnessed to the colonial mission elsewhere'. (Phillipson, 1992)

As language and culture are so closely interrelated, so inextricably bound together, the erasure of language signifies the erasure of culture, the values and beliefs that bind a people together. Language and culture play a central role in how we identify and provide a lens through which we can look back into our past. So, what happens when the indigenous language is erased and the international, universal language is placed beyond reach:

The majority of the time, English learned as a second language in public schools does not create a proficiency level adequate for working, studying, or relying on the language in daily life. Private language courses, summer exchange programs abroad and access to international schools are expensive and limited to a privileged minority. As is common, this kind of globalisation seems to only benefit the rich. (Corradi, 2017)

Ngũgĩ wa Thiong'o, the Kenyan writer and distinguished Professor, advocates that African writers also write in their mother tongues, because he understands how integral language is to a culture and its identity. Ngũgĩ wa Thiong'o's position is that since African literature is mostly written in the languages of the minority, the languages of the colonisers, this choice stifles the imagination of Africans and their propensity to be creative.

I remember my own creativity being stifled as a trainee student teacher back in 1979, in an example that I shared in Chap. 1, but is worth repeating here to illustrate a slightly different point. I had suggested to one of my lecturers that I do a comparative study between Wilfred Owen, an English poet, and Louise Bennett, a Jamaican poet, who wrote in patois. I was particularly interested in their respective views on the futility of war. My lecturer, while interested, suggested that I select a different author to Louise Bennett as 'there was no one here who could supervise this', 'here' being one of the Russell groups, considered to be a world-class university, that I was attending. Not only was my propensity to be creative while Black and Jamaican stifled, it signalled very clearly that the language of my education was no longer the language of my culture, which was, by the way, both English and patois. In addition to bringing to the forefront of my consciousness the fact that I didn't wish to be 'supervised', particularly in cultural matters where I was the burgeoning, 'expert', this conversation also highlighted that bringing my culture into that space was somehow delegitimising it as 'knowledge'. My culture was becoming redefined by my context as a form of resistance, because I was not prepared to give it up, to become 'educated'. I bought more books by Black writers in the 1980s, my first decade of teaching, than I did in all of the years combined since, and devoted myself to learning about my culture, my identity and what I legitimately brought to the table as a human being who was racialised Black.

As a Black educator training other Black educators, I was therefore cognisant that claims of language legitimacy work in tandem with education to delegitimise knowledge and perpetuate racial hierarchies of language. As Ngũgĩ wa Thiong'o (1994 [1986]) writes, 'colonial alienation starts with a deliberate disassociation of the language of conceptualisation, of thinking, of formal education, of mental development, from the language of daily interaction in the home and in the community' (p. 28). Colonial alienation, therefore, is a process that upholds the racial hierarchy of language and reproduces ideological perceptions in favour of English:

> English became the measure of intelligence and ability in the arts, the sciences and all the other branches of learning. English became the main determinant of child's progress up the ladder of formal education (wa Thiong'o 1994 [1986], p. 12). The above articulation of wa Thiong'o (1994 [1986]) highlights the privileged position afforded to English. It highlights the fact that English was not merely communicative; it was a marker of status, a barometer of intelligence, and an indicator of progress. (wa Thiong'o, 1994 [1986])

So, 'once the language of my education was no longer the language of my culture' to paraphrase wa Thiong'o, my culture in my case became my shield, to resist total assimilation to the point of oblivion, by my education. Like wa Thiong'o, I had no problem with writing in English, which is my mother tongue, and in fact love to this day many aspects of the English language. But I absolutely refuse to have English completely subsume the collective memory of my people that lives in patois for me, nor will I have patois delegitimised as an integral part of my personal and professional identity or knowledge, because it is beyond 'supervision'. The predecessor to Jamaican patois kept my ancestors alive in those cane fields as they plotted their escape. Label it vernacular, dialect, pidgin-English as you will, for me it will always convey much deeper meaning and connect me to my indigenous authentic self.

Current polemical discussions in the United Kingdom about the use of terms like 'BAME' and ethnic minorities are profoundly troubling. They are distracting as well as being outdated and therefore redundant. Part of the way in which people individually and collectively step into their power as authentic human beings is to be unambivalent about their identity, who they are and their connections to their roots. The current debates about terminology as they relate to race can leave the uninitiated confused, disempowered, disconnected and metaphorically 'on mute'.

Historically it has been white people, primarily white men, who hold the social, political and economic power to categorise people; this is no longer so. I further maintain that the terminology that refers to people who come from rich heritages and backgrounds that have contributed so much to shape the world, should befit the status of these people and the contribution made by their ancestors. Language should inspire a possibility to live into.

## 'BAME, PEOPLE OF COLOR, VISIBLE MINORITIES' AND OTHER PROVOCATIONS

Identity is complex and becoming increasingly so. Identity is nuanced and defined in a myriad of constantly evolving ways. Acronyms such as BAME, Black, Asian, Minority Ethnic, are not only clumsy and blunt but almost universally reviled by those so described. Besides which, BAME is becoming increasingly irrelevant due to its inaccuracy within a global and many local urban contexts where international migration patterns have changed the demographics of large West European cities dramatically. The acronym BAME is contentious but is still lazily, some would say intentionally, used across British government agencies and the media in the UK, thereby delegitimising the right that people so labelled have to self-identify or even 'be', on their terms. So, what does that say about the attitude of those who use the term towards racialised groups, and what does it say about racialised groups for allowing it?

Black leaders in America started to use the term 'People of Color' in the 1960s to describe African Americans; in 2020, we see the term expanded to include Latinos and Asian Americans. While seen by many as an empowering term that brings together and mobilises different ethnic groups towards common goals, which is to be applauded, 'People of Color' still situates whiteness as the norm. The challenge for me, therefore, with the acronym 'BAME' in the UK, the term 'People of Color' in the USA and 'visible minorities' in Canada, is that they all situate whiteness as the norm within their respective local contexts even when the opposite is true. Put another way, when you examine the fact that the experience of whiteness is not the norm for the majority of people on this planet, this is an undeniable truth.

Moving from the contexts of the global south, South America, Africa, India and China, to the large cities in Western Europe, the new majority is global and multi-lingual.

## White Minority

No exploration of racial categorisation would be complete without visiting Eurocentrism and whiteness within the social hierarchy. The kind of language and thinking that perpetuated racist ideology in the first place is subliminally effective in what it categorically states, who ignores, what it implies, how it subordinates, what and who it validates and what it elects to omit. Sustaining the concept of whiteness as a superior norm requires a denial of race, through 'white ignorance' as described by Mills in 2007.

Collective terms describing groups of people that share characteristics are fraught with difficulties, complexities and imperfections. Power structures, including the academy, tend to work in the interests of an elite minority. The elite, however, never define themselves as the minority that they are; they do not define themselves at all; they don't have to, they know who they are, and whom they have minoritised as outsiders. In this non-racialised space, the elite minority act with the confidence of a majority. These elites exist primarily, though not exclusively, through whiteness, and white ignorance—ignorance of race:

> Imagine an ignorance that resists. Imagine an ignorance that fights back. Imagine an ignorance militant, aggressive, not to be intimidated, an ignorance that is active, dynamic, that refuses to go quietly—not at all confined to the illiterate and uneducated but propagated at the highest levels of the land, indeed presenting itself unblushingly as knowledge. (Mills, 2007, p. 13)

This is how we experienced white supremacy, claiming to be ignorant about the endemic racism within the system, not seeing or acknowledging Black knowledge or experience, silently and militantly blaming the victims of the system, whether students or teachers, for their under-representation, under-achievement or over-exclusion.

The global minority certainly do not limit any notion of their identity to their numbers within a particular geographical location. The white elite act globally; their power has historically resided in large part in the fact that one per cent of the world's population holds approximately 44 per cent of the world's wealth. They are globally connected, operate collectively, in their mutually exclusive interest. They wield power accordingly, through transnational corporations, organisations, financial institutions, think-tanks, universities, governments and multi-nationals. Connected systems, economic, business, political, educational, health, all work with synchronised mindsets assiduously focused on maintaining the status quo for an elite minority, while simultaneously sowing and fuelling discord, disruption and distraction elsewhere, for the majority.

The elite minority are aided and abetted across the globe by those who are not white, but want desperately to appropriate whiteness to the extent that it is possible, or at least to share in the spoils. The 'third world', the occupied territory created for the global majority, is needed to maintain the concentration, flow and control of resources, wealth and power into the hands of the few, the global minority in the 'first world'. Poor whites are basic members of the white club, with minimal benefits; they are there to make up numbers when required and be the deflectors as they are currently being used in the divisive 'culture wars' in the UK; they are cannon-fodder and essentially act as the buffer between the white elite and those that the elite have 'othered'. The non-white allies are as intentional about joining the club as the elites are about maintaining the status quo and keeping them firmly at arm's length.

## Conclusion and Disrupting Narratives

A process of denial about systemic racism and white supremacy sustains deficit narratives.

For the status quo to be maintained, deficit narratives that play into centuries-old stereotypes about race need to be consistently perpetuated and reinforced. The media is central to this. Key to this approach is a language that minoritises, problematises, delegitimises and pathologises the Global Majority. At the same time, it eradicates or disregards their contributions and concerns. So, one does not need to be Einstein to understand that white people are the minority on the planet and that those people who are routinely referred to as 'ethnic minorities' are the hugely diverse Global Majority.

In 2003, when I first started using the term Global Majority, I was much more energised and inspired by the way Black and Asian educators across Britain reacted to, embraced and engaged with the collective and connecting term than I was about seeking permission to use it from a generally dismissive academy. On this occasion their indifference assisted me. The praxis that evolved from that confidence of a majority perspective not only changed the face of school leadership in cities such as London, but its heart:

> The pleas for more black people to be represented in senior leadership positions and to be among the decision-makers in public institutions, particularly in schools and children's services, should be accompanied by the determination to embrace their additionality, and enable them to create where needed, different more nuanced ways of leading. If form follows function, then the accompanying changes in organisational cultures and structures are another bonus of their arrival. (Campbell-Stephens, 2009, pp. 321–333)

Correctly describing the Global Majority as such moves the conversation away from disadvantage to advantage, and the added value, what I call the 'additionality', that these groups of rich, diverse heritages potentially bring (Portelli & Campbell-Stephens 2009). Additionality speaks to the fact that Black leadership at its best is unsurpassed and has been exemplary in many spectacular global incidences in elevating the human condition. Imagine embracing being Black as a distinct advantage, a badge of excellence.

So, as a programme designer addressing under-representation, using a critical-race lens provided me with an alternative and liberating filter for the language, concepts and content of that programme in 2003. The course was intentionally focused on changing educational leadership praxis as having better representation was not enough: we wanted leaders who could bring their authentic selves into the leadership space, thereby irretrievably, radically, changing it. But we started by challenging those leaders:

> What difference does it make to the situation of the majority of the group such Black staff are supposed to represent, if the training and professional socialization those Black staff receive, the institutional culture of which they are a part and the systems and processes they operate are identical to that of their white counterparts? (John, 2009)

The intention that the call for more leaders from diverse backgrounds should be accompanied by the predisposition to create spaces, through professional development, that enabled those leaders to use their difference to make a difference was one that we intentionally foregrounded in the leadership training. As Dei points out, 'Inclusion is not about bringing people into what already exists; it is about creating a new space, a better space for everyone' (Dei, 2000, pp. 111–132).

Power is inextricably linked to majority status even when, statistically, the group holding power is the minority: if their language is the language of authority, intelligence, wisdom, then that's the language that holds power. While some of the public conversations about race, post-2020, are among the most candid there have ever been, the fact remains that there is denial about systemic anti-Black racism being deeply embedded and woven throughout the fabric of Western societies. There is also a collective amnesia, silence, but periodic co-ordinated push back that all indicate white supremacy and fragility in the same breath. The liberal push to prioritise diversity and inclusion entails not talking about race or the power dynamics that exist between diverse groups. How does inclusion into a repressive system work in the conscious Black person's interest? When there is any progress towards addressing racism, the system's intentional shift in language over the decades is a familiar ploy. The subsequent move will be to make the focus on race the problem, especially when it is pitted against other systemic inequalities such as class. So, the inequality suffered by the 'disadvantaged', proxy for 'working-class', will be positioned as being the real victim, now portrayed as being ignored, marginalised or worsened because of a focus on race.

Language is weaponised and deployed, particularly after pivotal historical moments such as equality legislation being passed, any substantive progress on Civil Rights, the Black Power Movement, or after various iterations of Black Lives Matters. The language deployed serves to push back, distract from, undermine, gaslight, and in other ways, halt or reverse any steps forward towards racial equality. Following the shift in language comes the decisive and direct change of policy, backwards.

This book contends that one of the reasons that so little has changed fundamentally over decades is that much of the discourse on diversity and inclusion serves to avoid talking explicitly about race and the impact of racism on people's real lives. The diversity and inclusion narrative skirts around race issues and stops short of identifying structural anti-Black racism instead of more comfortable representation and inclusion options.

Narrative should enable the articulation of a human voice from which we might recognise ourselves and our global humanity. Mignolo (2009) reminds us that the role of the socially conscious scholar is to strive towards a humanising epistemology.

## REFERENCES

African Narrative. (2020, October 29). *YouTube: The day Nelson Mandela conquered America/Your enemy is not my enemy/Mandela in America.*

Campbell-Stephens, R. (2009, July). Investing in diversity: Changing the face (and the heart) of educational leadership. *School Leadership and Management, 29*(3), 321–333.

Cesaire, A. (1972). *Discourse on colonialism.* Monthly Review Press.

Corradi, A. (2017). The linguistic colonialism of English. *The Brown Political Review.*

Dei, G. J. S. (2000). Rethinking the role of indigenous knowledges in the academy. *International Journal of Inclusive Education, 4*(2), 111–132.

John, G. (2009). *Investing in diversity conference, After-dinner speeches 2003–2010.*

Migge, B., & Léglise, I. (2007). *Creoles in education: An appraisal of current programs and projects P337.* John Benjamins Publishing Company.

Mignolo, (2009). Epistemically Disobedience, Independent Thought and De-colonial Freedom. *Theory, Culture & Society, 26*(7–8), 1–23 (SAGE, Los Angeles, London, New Delhi, and Singapore), https://doi.org/10.1177/0263276409349275

Mills, C. W. (2007). White ignorance. In *Race and epistemologies* (pp. 13–38). State University of New York.

Phillipson, R. (1992). *Linguistic imperialism.* Oxford University Press.

Phillipson, R. (2001). *Cultural conceptualisations in West African English; A cognitive-linguistic approach* (pp. 241, 290, 294). Peter Lang.

Phillipson, R. (2008). *The Routledge handbook of world Englishes* (p. 678). Routledge.

Portelli, J. P., & Campbell-Stephens, R. (2009). *Leading for equity: The investing in diversity approach.* Edphil Books.

Roche, G. (2019). Articulating language oppression: Colonialism, coloniality and the erasure of Tibet's minority languages. *Patterns of Prejudice, 53*(5), 487–514. https://doi.org/10.1080/0031322X.2019.1662074

Smith, P. (2021). *Presentation entitled Rac(e)ing toward language for children in a 'post-colonial' Caribbean.* Shortwood Teacher's College.

wa Thiong'o, N. (1994 [1986]). *Decolonising the mind: The politics of language in African literature.* James Currey.

# CHAPTER 4

# Seven Women, Seven Steps: Consciousness and Collective Action

**Abstract** This chapter highlights how the transition from minoritised status to majority identity for Black educators relies on a search for authenticity and how, through developing an Afrocentric consciousness, projects of resistance provide enriching opportunities for being. The chapter examines how an opportunity to disrupt deficit narratives and demonstrate efficacy was liberating, normal and relatively uncomplicated through indigenous 'we' orientated collective action. Essentially this is a short story of seven women who, in their search for an explicit expression of authenticity, found sisterhood while utilising womanist activism to save a school from closure. The chapter explores how a relearning of indigenous forms of being, such as Ubuntu, found successful expression in strategic implementation. It addresses the importance of racial affinity and cultural literacy as well as competence. It concludes with seven steps to consciousness.

**Keywords** Collective leadership • Activism • Women leaders • Ubuntu

The legacies of colonialism include an agonising search for authenticity by individuals and cultures (Fanon, 1963), as well as projects of resistance that include a relearning of indigenous forms of being itself (Mignolo, 2009).

© The Author(s), under exclusive license to Springer Nature Switzerland AG 2021
R. M. Campbell-Stephens, *Educational Leadership and the Global Majority*, https://doi.org/10.1007/978-3-030-88282-2_4

65

## DEVELOPING CONSCIOUSNESS

The relationship between power, ideology, discourse and what passes as systems of knowledge in the West is perhaps nowhere more evident than classifications and hierarchies based on race (Anderson, 1991). As Stoler (1995) argues, power organises knowledge in a way that justifies and reproduces historical, social and racial distinctions and exclusions in the world. It is those who experience the effects of these classifications, who have distinct ways of knowing, that are continuously marginalised in the dominant, mainstream, Western scholarly canon of epistemology.

The process of being racialised, minoritised and placed at the bottom of a hierarchy where white people sit at the top ensured that some of the educators from these groups, were highly susceptible to internalising racism (Woodson, 1933; Freire, 1970; Hooks, 1995). Nowhere within initial teacher training, middle or senior leadership training or ongoing professional development thereafter were there any opportunities or safe spaces to unpack the way in which teachers from Black and Minority Ethnic (BME) backgrounds were socialised into their professional identities through their training in the UK. Individual discriminatory acts can be addressed, although the cost on wellbeing and mental health of consistently reacting to micro-aggressions or worse should not be underestimated. It is the structural, institutional impacts of racialisation that rot your soul, diminishing, minoritising and 'othering' the racialised individual, their community, undermining identity and invalidating contribution and knowledge. A relearning of your indigenous self for Black and other Global Majority people is not part of the narrative of inclusion and diversity. There is a subtle assimilation process, where experiences are deracialised and therefore not seen or heard. Recognition, acceptance, belonging , validation are the rewards awaiting the non-white. Structural barriers such as racism, including assumptions about capabilities based on racial/ethnic stereotypes, are everyday experiences for BME teachers, supposedly unseen by the white establishment.

So, just as the teachers' experiences are invisible, so are the barriers, creating suspicion and speculation when the question is posed about why BME teachers are unable to progress their careers beyond a certain level. There are doubts about BME teachers' confidence, capabilities and competence, and this is borne out apparently by their under-representation within the system, especially at senior levels. Some of what I have observed as a practitioner over many years may evade researchers exploring the

BME teacher's experience, because some teachers will find it difficult to describe the more covert subtle types of interactions in which they are left othered, wondering or both. The overwhelming pressures to assimilate will have been such that while identifying as 'minorities', to fit in, not pose a threat or a challenge, they may not have been positively able to identify as Black, African, African Caribbean or Asian. Hooks (1994) describes the colonised mind as being 'self-oppressing' and speaks to the intersections of 'gender expression, race, culture, sexual identity and class' as being seen by the oppressed as inferior. The latter, Hooks explains,

> requires diverse peoples as a matter of social and organizational policy to assimilate into the dominant group values and attitudes, and negate their diversity, and imitate Euro-Americans and their way of life. The use of the term Euro-American is itself a marker of ethnicity, a deprivileging of the white supremacist idea that everyone else but whites has ethnicity. (Hooks, 1994, p. 43; Hooks, 1995, pp. 31–33)

This pressure to assimilate as a minority is also true within a professional UK context, with a racist culture and white values that is dependent on not seeing, yet simultaneously, racialising 'minorities' as BME. All of this while denying that systemic racism even exists. Ethnic minority, minority ethnic, whichever way expressed—those so described are made 'less than', and they face the associated negative connotations that accompany minority status. The process of racial minoritisation is a social process shaped by power:

> Terms like 'ethnic minorities' are not neutral phrases referring to population size. Simplistic views like this ignore the central role of power. In South Africa, white people are a cultural majority despite being the numerical minority. (Selvarajah et al., 2020)

The commonality of the way in which systemically racist power structures operate globally needs to be analysed and understood, not just within separate distinct groups, but as part of the way in which we come to understand more generally how globally numerical majorities become racialised as minorities. These Global Majority communities have had their collective cultural, economic, political and social power eroded to varying degrees, subordinating them to a perceived norm outside of which they

68    R. M. CAMPBELL-STEPHENS

exist. In part, this erasure takes place through the targeting and labelling of identity, in ways that sustain structures of hegemony.

Connecting peoples of the Global Majority with their knowledge, narratives and ways of being and each other potentially contributes to a globalisation of a different kind, one that is not driven by the economic greed of the minority, but by the social needs of the majority. If the social needs of the Global Majority community are prioritised,

> then the condition of globality, in revealing the interdependence of peoples, and the fundamental social and historical linkages that have always existed between societies (Wolf, 1982), even if they have often been unacknowledged, can potentially provoke a more authentic, liberatory and just vision of human community.

This is why market-driven global economies that command that the world be organised for competition and exploitation in the name of profit, can no longer be tolerated by the majority as the dominant global narrative. Marketisation, neo-liberalism, commoditisation and add to that eugenics-based policy, because it is economically driven, reduce education to the utilitarian skills for work, instead of education 'for the social good with intrinsic value' Lopez (2020). In addition, a move away from a colonial 'I' orientation to a more humanistic 'we' orientation is critical. Fanon (1963) challenges the colonial concept of individualism. He describes decolonisation as a 'profound social reorganisation', one that requires brotherhood, sisterhood and comradeship.

## SEVEN WOMEN

Like the American abolitionist and women's rights activist Sojourner Truth, I have found it impossible for my race and gender to be separated. And as with the American feminist author Bell Hooks, class too has to be a part of the conversation, as do caste, colour and colourism and how these have impacted the interactions between dark and light-skinned Black and Asian women. The following story falls into the Black feminist tradition that is activist grounded in lived experiences. These lived experiences of racism, sexism and classism are inseparable all must be addressed simultaneously.

Reorganisation and subversion of the dominant narrative was what an unlikely group of change-makers successfully came together to do in

2013. Seven busy women, who decided to journey together, starting with the end in mind, dared to construct an alternative narrative to that of the dominant culture, and in doing so, created their own kind of 'fugitive pedagogy' (Givens, 2021) for supporting and reviving a vulnerable school serving a Black community. They came together intentionally, invited by and inviting each other, for a purpose that required a collective communal consciousness, which they co-created, with urgency.

We are taught that our relationships with one another diminish rather than enrich our experience. We are taught that women are 'natural' enemies, that solidarity will never exist between us because we cannot, should not, and do not bond with one another. We have learned these lessons well. We must unlearn them if we are to build a sustained feminist movement. We must learn to live and work in solidarity. We must learn the true meaning and value of Sisterhood (Hooks, 1986).

It is because so little in the early writings of feminist theory expands on women's experiences of 'unlearning' and practising solidarity and sisterhood that I have included this brief but perfectly formed decolonising narrative. The main protagonists are women, six Black and one white. They are not the victims, but the victors, and their version of sisterhood was rooted in their lived experiences and their understandings of reality and that of their female African ancestors prior to and independent of racial oppression.

Moreover, as a result of colonialism, imperialism, slavery, apartheid and other systems of racial domination, Black people share a common experience of oppression. These two factors foster shared Afrocentric values that permeate the family structure, religious institutions, culture and community life of Blacks in varying parts of Africa, the Caribbean, South America and North America. This Afrocentric consciousness permeates the shared history of people of African descent through the framework of a distinctive Afrocentric epistemology (Collins, 1990).

A small Christian, voluntary-aided school of historical significance to the Black community in the UK, hereafter referred to as 'School C' was placed in special measures in 2013. Special measures was an inspection category that indicated that the school was in serious need of support and vulnerable to closure by Ofsted the UK schools inspectorate. At the time, School C was deemed inadequate in all four inspection categories. A series of school improvement and interim headteachers had been dispatched into the school by the local authority over nine months, to no avail. The school slipped further and further into trouble. With teachers leaving, the governing body and headteacher removed, and a growing deficit, parents began to remove their children. Even the church community seemed to have lost hope in their little, but once well-loved, school. With a local authority under scrutiny by the Department for Education, one more small failing primary school looked as though it were about to go under.

The call for help could not personally have come at a worse time for the interim chair of governors, as plans for her to emigrate were in the advanced stages. Likewise for other members of the team, the timing was stress-inducing because of everything else going on in their lives. All of that said, the call, in equal parts, because of who it was from, and what it was about, could not be ignored. In the same year that School C had been placed in special measures, a sister secondary school in a different part of the country had closed, and the community was in deep mourning for a school that at one time was a beacon of excellence for the Black community. School C could not go the same way. The seven women came together and built a liberatory framework for working collectively in the interests of the school community to which they were all in different ways connected and invested. They were determined not to fail, even against the backdrop of a politically hostile environment and the very many competing priorities going on in their lives. Swimming upstream all the way, they set off on their adventure together, back to a version of their ancestral selves.

The deficit narratives problematising and conflating education within majority Black contexts with failure had to be disrupted. Ironically, through a neo-liberal lens, all of the women had either something to directly gain from the school closure, or from another perspective, if successful, something to lose. The seven women included the head of the Teaching School Alliance (School A); the headteacher and the deputy headteacher of School B, commissioned by the Teaching School Alliance to support School C; the interim headteacher of the failing school (School C); the chair of governors and the clerk to governors, both elected by the Local Education Authority (LEA) to form an interim governing body, essentially to oversee School C's closure, although this was never explicitly stated.

An invitation, immediately from the very first conversation, became a provocation. The invitation came from the seventh woman to the woman that she invited to chair the interim governing body. The invitation provided an opportunity for both women to plan, but more importantly, act. Starting with the end in mind, that is, School C out of special measures, within a broader family of schools, retaining its distinctive Black Christian ethos, a detailed plan was hatched. The plan's success hinged on a number of factors, but key was the relational intelligence that existed within the team. Every single move was considered as if it were a chess championship and the roles of the women as if they were chess pieces. Among other things, they believed that together they could achieve their goal, but it required forensic focus, and a commitment to sleep after the work was done. All women were experienced educators and school leaders. This was the first time, however, that the chair of governors, who was previously a local authority adviser, an Ofsted inspector and a secondary school head-teacher before becoming a consultant to the Department for Education and the National College for School leadership, had been a chair of governors. The clerk to the governors was not only highly experienced in governance but had many years previously also been a parent with a child at School C. For her this was personal; she went on to establish a national network for Black school governors. These women were in their different ways personally invested in seeing this school not just survive but thrive, and they were prepared, unlike real chess pieces, to be individually agile, shifting position as needed, sometimes pawn, at others a rook, and occasionally as the queen.

At the first of many meetings, it was decided that the mission for that team would not be to oversee the closure of the school. This took courage and was a first step towards the collective consciousness that they would go on to forge; the decision deliberately took them into 'fugitive' territory. This decision was not noted in the minutes of meetings or communicated in any formal way to the local authority until the school's long-term future had been secured: all warfare, according to the military strategist Sun Tsu, is based on deception (Sun Tsu, sixth century BC).

The Ubuntu (Nguni Bantu for 'humanity') approach to collective leadership assisted these professionals to face the challenge from a 'we' as opposed to an 'I' orientation. In working through this process over a twelve-month period, strategies were developed to engage with the various stakeholders in a culturally respectful, intelligent but pragmatic manner. This required careful planning. Attention to detail was critical as was occasionally going against the prevailing wisdom about not 'over-thinking'. In some situations, the strategy, to appear weak or at least understated, so as to entice the opponent into a false sense of security played dividends. The opposition, while writing their opponents off as unworthy, displayed their hand with the usual arrogance. The timing of the various steps of the process was precisely synchronised to within days, sometimes hours, of parallel activities happening elsewhere within the system which were designed to do the exact opposite of what the women were aiming to achieve. These strategies, essentially of moving consciousness into planned action, were executed with precision. Oftentimes the stance was offensive, challenging the church or local authority, but always being one step ahead. At other times it was side-stepping or avoidance. At still other times it required acting like a deep-sea submarine, operating under the radar.

The practice of Ubuntu beyond the context of this one school, for example, encouraged the Teaching School Alliance (School A) that was led by one of the team to be braver in developing womanist models of leadership from lived experience. This meant being braver about inviting Black professionals to create their leadership narratives and models, from their perspectives, to act collectively, to be humanist and explicit about what they legitimately brought to the school improvement table and leadership piece, by virtue of who they are, not in spite of it.

Inevitably, there was some resistance to some of the team's strategies, especially from those elements of the local authority with which the team had to engage, and even within some sections of the community itself. Distractions were kept within peripheral vision, but at arm's length. The shift from reacting to activism created an empowering space in which to think, plan and work. It was nurturing to the soul and the intellect. To be so disruptive in plain sight was frankly exhilarating as well. The space in that context was reliant on dimming the white gaze, to the level of a haze, while creating an environment where the women could work authentically. There were two occasions in my career where I experienced something similar. The first was while co-running a Pan-African supplementary school over a ten-year period and simultaneously holding various other mainstream roles. The second occasion was while leading the Investing in Diversity leadership programme at University College London for eight years.

Whiteness, reacting to whiteness, resisting whiteness, was not the focus during these periods. This was one of the key learning points in doing strategic level work, the need to relegate to a secondary position the wider white environment and reactions to it. Certainly, always keep that broader political context in peripheral vision, but don't focus on it. Instead, understand those components of detail, like the Ofsted visit, that can leave you dead in the water, and retain forensic focus on the time scales for getting any required documentation and procedures completed and in place. Begin with the end in mind, and in focus.

Ultimately, paying attention internally was a priority as there was much to do that went beyond window-dressing, and could only be seen by those within. Rebuilding community and securing the internal foundations, that could withstand inspectors' scrutiny was more important in this intervention year than reacting to the wider system's racism. Replacing the decaying infrastructure, structurally within the physical building, as well as systemically within the school's functions and processes, were key to securing staff belief and retaining parents' patience. What was different in the 'We' orientation as opposed to 'I' was the lack of arrogance, the absence of the mentality of the overseer, and the belief that the very real problems in the school could be overcome over the long term. There was also a restoration of memory about the role that the school had played within that community and the critical role that it could play into the future. Just by the team being there, it intimated to the Black community what was possible. But it required some radical reimagining.

Not having to explain actions to defensive white colleagues, beyond the monthly meetings with the local authority colleagues and the periodic Ofsted visits, conserved much needed energy and alleviated one area of stress, although there were many more. Unapologetic racial and cultural awareness and affinity within the seven-woman team extended to the wider governing body and the wider community, saved time, provided consensus and established a foundation on which to build trust and bring genuine challenge. People who had the requisite skills, aptitudes and dispositions were essential as there was no time to train up colleagues to become culturally competent. People were needed who arrived Black and could hit the ground running hard. Challenge, when offered, while not always welcomed, was respected.

The Teaching School Alliances ongoing professional development offer was enriched by the experiences of the team. Authentic leaders training for aspiring Black school leaders was offered as a result. This approach to professional development deliberately moved training away from the mechanics of being a colour-blind educator, in a systemically racist system, to being an authentic Black leader working in the interests of the community you served. And School C was a real live case study. The preoccupation was not to assimilate into a system that diminished, but to navigate that system in order to deconstruct and build a space where our knowledge could be utilised. Once again, the liberatory inspiration of the Brazilian educator Paulo Freire was at the forefront of consciousness. Black educators' purpose was enhanced by enabling them to legitimately bring their expertise, knowledge and lived experience as Black people to their professional identities and the way they led, without white validation or otherwise. My best work over forty years has been in precisely spaces like these, which is why it was critical to understand how to create them.

The model of leadership employed was steeped in the African Ubuntu philosophy centred on personhood, morality, social and political activism. The typical expression of connectedness or collective personhood undermined the drive that there might have been to competitiveness between the schools and the individuals involved:

> Samkange and Samkange (1980) highlight the three maxims of hunhuism or Ubuntuism. The first maxim asserts that to be human is to affirm one's humanity by recognising the humanity of others and, on that basis, establish respectful human relations with them. And the second maxim means that if and when one is faced with a decisive choice between wealth and the preservation of the life of another human being, then one should opt for the preservation of life. The third maxim as a principle deeply embedded in traditional African political philosophy says that the king owed his status, including all the powers associated with it, to the will of the people under him.

So, the model required that the stakeholders be actively participatory in a collective interest. None of the seven women wanted to see School C close, although had it done so, both Schools A and B would have 'benefitted', viewing the situation though a neo-liberal Western lens. To explain, School B was a good and rapidly improving school on an upward trajectory, with smart leadership, on an extensive site, with surplus capacity. School B, brokered in by the head of the Teaching School Alliance, could easily have stood back and waited for School C to fold, as because of their geographical proximity to each other and existing student demographic, School B could have taken all of School C's 196 children and instantly become a large two-form entry school. Instead, the head and deputy of School B fought for over twelve months for the survival of the troubled school. The decision between growing their empire and preservation of School C came down to preservation. Both the headteacher and the deputy of school B spent at least four days a week between them in School C for an entire academic year, routinely putting in twelve- to eighteen-hour days, while still running their school. Incredibly, School B gained an outstanding inspection grade in all categories the week following School C's inspection, which took it out of measures and away from imminent closure.

In March 2015, nearly two years after going into special measures and twelve months after the Ubuntu-inspired intensive intervention was implemented, School C was brought out of special measures. Leadership and management were deemed 'good'; the three other categories required improvement. The school is now a stand-alone sponsored academy that has retained its distinctive Christian ethos, within the family of the Anglican Diocese, which is its sponsor. It is now an exemplar in the city for the work that it has done and continues to do on decolonising its curriculum content, a phenomenally exceptional achievement by any standard.

The attributes displayed by these women were those of leaders with moral purpose who believed in their collective mission. The glue that held them together was the imperative to save the school for their community, a community in which they were personally invested the Black community. The leadership attributes, by their admission, included being servant leaders, stewards, architects, activists, advocates, coaches and storytellers, supported by high dosages of cultural and racial affinity, ethical, cultural and relational intelligence, rooted in trust and love.

The women began by coming to terms with who they were as people, leveraging their identity, their values, identifying their purpose, and embracing simultaneously their ways of being and seeing. Seven women from different backgrounds used those backgrounds to inform their approach to leadership. A deep-rooted ethic of responsibility not just to their peers, but a strong sense of being connected to the narratives of the communities they serve, is the traditional African way. A heightened sense of moral purpose, an affinity for leadership, focused on relationships and collective action and a conviction to collective responsibility defined their stewardship and contributed heavily to the writing of their narrative.

The polyrhythms in African-American music, in which no one main beat subordinates the others, is paralleled by the theme of individual expression in Black women's quilting. Black women quilters place strong colour and patterns next to one another and see the individual differences not as detracting from each piece but as enriching the whole quilt Collins (1990).

The magnet that initially pulled these system leaders together was the understanding of the historical importance of the school, not just to the Adventist Community, but also to the wider Black community. This was especially important given the colossal loss of the 'sister secondary school' in another city a few years earlier, which was at one time a beacon school for the whole community. While the local authority had brokered in various levels of high-powered support for School C, following the usual formula for struggling schools, clearly there was ambivalence or dishonesty about the real intention for the school's future, because the persistent and consistent narrative among council officers was that it would close. More than likely, the women concerned would have been viewed as the perfect scapegoats, exposed as they all were on the narrow glass ledge. More than anything, the seven women knew that they could turn that school around, and against the odds they did.

And what of the white female ally who in many ways became a catalyst, by approaching first the head of the Teaching School Alliance and the interim chair of governors? Well, the timing in this instance was absolutely key. One of the reasons that a similar intervention failed with the sister school was that by the time the call to action was put out it was too late. Invitations to be involved, received in December over the Christmas holiday, when the school closed twelve weeks later in March, was much too late.

The one white female ally in this situation embodied white allyship at its best, without being the white saviour. First, she nailed her colours to the mast in her initial conversations with the two women whom she approached as her allies: the chair of governors and the head of the Teaching School Alliance and School A. She saw allyship as a two-way process. She was going to fight to keep that school open, with or without the help of the Black colleagues that she approached. She stated her reasons as a white woman for wanting that Black school to survive and hoped that there would be sufficient synergy between her reasons and her potential allies to work together. Each of the three women knew each other in separate relationships going back many years. They knew, respected and, importantly, trusted each other. Their skill sets complimented each other. One was not a practising Christian for example, but was an activist, and both of the other two women were Christians within the Anglican Diocese and could navigate that terrain with relative ease.

The seventh woman also used her senior position, her leverage and access to act at both a strategic and personal level. She advocated to have key people in place and then stepped back, having no further say as to who else would be brought in or how the team would work. She ensured, leading from the back, that barriers to things that needed to be done would be lowered if not removed, by having conversations with her colleagues to which the team were not privy. The team sought her counsel, as she sought theirs, and the team ensured that anything done reflected well on her, as she was rightly highly respected in education and within the Anglican church and therefore needed to be protected. This kind of allyship could not be taken for granted. Many tears were shed because of the personal toll that the work took. This white woman's Irish roots, as well as her activism, earned her the right to be counted as the seventh womanist.

Below are seven of the many steps to consciousness that the women took on their particular journey together (Karenga, 2002).

## Step One: Remembering and Rejuvenating. Harmony

One of the impacts of colonisation, old and new, is that through the erasure of memory, the spirit to resist domination and an imposed world view that ultimately becomes the norm in hearts and minds, is eroded. A wholistic remembering of who one is, through ancestry, is critical. Indigenous knowledge, aligned to indigenous ways of thinking, seeing and being, is essential to rejuvenating capabilities and re-establishing agency. This returning to self within the community of others brings harmony, through listening, hearing and responding to self and others. Where there is synergy between deeply held values and what you do professionally contributes to harmony with self and the community.

## Step Two: Decolonising the Mind: Developing a Collective Black Consciousness—Order and Self-determination

For the women the first stage of the decolonising process was in this particular instance to decolonise their approach to their relationships with each other, and exercise self-control, openness and patience. There were no hierarchies based on status or class, no egos based on titles or job roles, just roles and responsibilities, focused on one outcome. Black consciousness is critical to liberation of the colonised African mind. A consciousness with heightened levels of racial awareness invites affinity and unity. Being locked into a constant struggle of resistance to white supremacy undermines the capacity to radically reimagine a Black consciousness. Decolonisation requires a reset of the cognitive mindset which positions

Black and Brown people as being less than white people, thereby creating a space where they can become self-determining and define who they are as Black and Global Majority people. By embracing the way in which their identities influence and strengthen their capacity to make a difference in any given situation, they are embracing a version of self that is focused on *being* instead of being focused on reacting. This approach brought an order to the way in which these women approached business.

## STEP THREE: UBUNTU AND BEING CONNECTED—
## LEADERSHIP AS SERVICE

The social ethic of Ubuntu should be listed as one of Africa's greatest contributions to a disconnected ego-centric world. Ubuntu is the essence of being human and connected. Desmond Tutu, one of the philosophy's biggest proponents, further stated that the quality of Ubuntu gives people resilience, enabling them to survive and emerge still human despite all efforts to dehumanise them (Tutu 2000). His view is that in African ontology, Ubuntu symbolises the backbone of African spirituality. Working from the 'We' orientation as opposed to the 'I', we reconnect first of all with ourselves and what it is to be human and then connect to others. Ubuntu relates to bonding with others. This is in line with what the word expresses in most African languages: being self because of others. This is also in line with the popular Zulu saying: *Ubuntu ngumuntu ngabantu* (I am because we are). Such sayings as I am because we are and I am human because I belong, express this tenet. This means that in African philosophy, an individual is human if he or she says I participate, therefore I am. In Western aphorism, Hailey (2008) argued that the individual is expected to say 'I think, therefore I am':

> This belief in connectedness and the use of dialogue as one of its criteria for methodological adequacy has Afrocentric roots. In contrast to Western either/or dichotomous thought, the traditional African world view is holistic and seeks harmony. 'One must understand that to become human, to realise the promise of becoming human, is the only important task of the person,' posits Molefi Asante. People become more human and empowered only in the context of a community, and only when they 'become seekers of the type of connections, interactions, and meetings that lead to harmony.' As Collins (1990) points out the power of the word generally, and dialogues specifically, allows this to happen. (Collins, 1990)

## STEP FOUR: FINDING YOUR AUTHENTIC VOICE AND NARRATIVE-CARRYING PURPOSE

It is hugely liberating and inspiring to understand that for millennia, before globalisation, white supremacy, colonisation and capitalism, there were people who lived by different paradigms. Developing an authentic Global Majority mindset and lens enables a different version of globalisation to be conceived, one for example, where lived experiences of oppression promote orientations towards equity and social justice and are seen as normal, desirable and humane. Conceptualising through the prism of the Global Majority starting from where and who you are, instead of looking at yourself through a mirror darkly as minoritised minorities, takes you firmly into authenticity territory. Narratives are also key to building consciousness. In order to effectively pass on narratives in any culture, one has to do so authentically. Narratives as autobiography, particularly for those who have never been at the centre of their story, are powerful. Finding community where you can create such narratives and pass on the blueprint, is as good as passing on generational wealth.

## STEP FIVE: RELATIONAL INTELLIGENCE COMBINED WITH RACIAL AFFINITY

A heightened sense of relational intelligence as Black women underpinned the way that the team worked together. It helped that they felt that they had been brought together for a higher purpose and that it was destined that they were sitting together. Racial affinity provided a space of belonging, affirming, respectful challenge, support, love and occasional shade. It provided a space where the women did not have to educate white people, navigate white hostility or fragility, or explain certain situations that they all understood.

## STEP SIX: BEING CULTURALLY COMPETENT

Being culturally competent should be an essential criterion for any leader anywhere. The ability to read, understand and interact across cultures is critical in a globally diverse world. Equally important for effective leadership that is not reliant on the one superhero leader is the ability to coach those that you lead in building cultural competence and resilience. It requires humility, a knowing where previously there was a 'not knowing', seeing or even acknowledgement. Being more adept at reading the cultural contexts and demonstrating a kind of cultural dexterity as well as competence are all highly desirable leadership qualities in diverse contexts.

## STEP SEVEN: CONSCIOUS COLLECTIVE ACTION AND RESPONSIBILITY

Recognising that you have collective power as Black people is rare in educational settings within the West. All the people involved knew that their lived experiences of oppression, and conversely, success, blended to build their resiliency, adaptability and flexibility and added to their ability to attend to contextual issues of power and relationships within the team. They also felt that they were attuned to the voices that were frequently unrepresented, as well as the voices of those that were missing. Their responsibility to each other and the contract that they had crafted between themselves and the wider community, was as strong a bond as they needed.

## CONCLUSION

I had worked in education for twenty years as a teacher, school inspector, headteacher and government adviser before coming to this leadership work eighteen years ago. Therefore, I know from lived experience that many Black or Asian teachers who had committed to being activists to change the system were tired of being othered, problematised, ignored or conversely, relentlessly subjected to the surveillance of the white gaze in a system that claimed to be colour-blind. The concept of operating through the lens of being a part of the Global Majority unleashes from a minority mindset those that have been minoritised by white supremacy. It invites the Global Majority to take their rightful place locally, regionally and globally to, if not co-create with other movements, the post-colonial world order, then certainly take intentional steps towards it. As Bell Hooks describes it through her writings, 'teaching to transgress.' Operating as a member of the Global Majority is liberating and empowering, but as Lopez (2020) reminds us, decolonisation is a process. This chapter is intended to make a small contribution to illuminating that process in one specific context.

The model of leadership co-created in the story of the seven women foregrounds the ethnic, cultural, social and life experiences of those educators and how these intersections legitimately shaped their professional identities. The knowledge of Black professionals is routinely ignored, appropriated or adulterated within a knowledge apartheid that has a hierarchy, upholding Western knowledge as simultaneously superior, neutral and universal. So, while some Black and other Global Majority educators do occupy leadership positions, being fully present or finding their authentic voice often requires a level of epistemic disobedience (Mignolo, 2009), even in contexts where they are the majority.

The importance of leaders decolonising their thinking first cannot be overestimated. A cognitive resetting is needed before attention is turned to practice. While more easily said than done, I think that such a process is now well within the realms of possibility. Strobel (1997) contends that decolonisation of the mind is a process of reconnecting with the past to understand the present—like the mythical African Sankofa bird, returning to reclaim that which was lost, but is critical to moving forward.

## References

Anderson, K. J. (1991). *Vancouver's Chinatown: Racial discourse in Canada, 1875–1980*. McGill-Queen's University Press.

Collins, P. (1990). *Black feminist thought: Knowledge, consciousness, and the politics of empowerment, by permission of the publisher*. Routledge.

Fanon, F. (1963). The wretched of the earth (C. Farrington, Trans.). Grove Press

Freire, I. (1970). *Pedagogy of the oppressed*. The Continuum International Publishing Group Inc..

Givens, J. (2021). *Fugitive pedagogy, Carter G. Woodson and the art of black teaching. Woodson and the art of black teaching*. Harvard University Press.

Hailey, J. (2008). Ubuntu: A literature review commissioned by the Tutu Foundation in the UK

Hooks, B. (1986). Sisterhood: Political solidarity between Women. *Feminist Review 1986, 23*(1), 125–138.

Hooks, B. (1994). *Teaching to transgress: Education as the practice of freedom*. Routledge.

Hooks, B. (1995). *Killing rage: Ending racism*. Henry Holt & Co..

Karenga, M. (2002). *Introduction to Black studies. Kawaida philosophy* (pp. 311–314). The University of Sankore Press.

Lopez, A. (2020). *Decolonising educational leadership: Exploring alternative approaches to leading schools*. Palgrave Macmillan.

Mignolo, W. (2009). Epistemic disobedience, independent thought and decolonial freedom. Theory, Culture & Society

Samkange and Samkange. (1980). *Hunhuism or Ubuntuism: A Zimbabwe indigenous political philosophy.* Graham Publishers.

Selvarajah, S., Deivanayagam, T. A., & Lasco, G. (2020). Categorisation and minoritisation. *BMJ Global Health, 5,* e004508. https://doi.org/10.1136/bmjgh-2020-004508

Stoler, A. L. (1995). *Race and the education of desire: Foucault's history of sexuality and the colonial order of things.* Duke University Press.

Strobel, E. (1997). Coming full circle: The process of decolonization among post-1965 Filipino Americans. Publisher??

Wolf, E. (1982). *Europe and the people without history.* University of California Press.

Woodson, C. (1933). The Mis-education of the Negro. *Journal of American History, 20*(2), 1.

# CHAPTER 5

# Culturally Competent Leadership

**Abstract** This chapter provides a new contextual lens to reimagine educational leadership in the context of a Covid-19 world where Black lives *do* matter. Resting on the notion, as Lopez (2020) reminds us, that 'communities and educators have knowledge', opportunities to draw on all relevant knowledge in support of decolonising educational leadership could pull schools and communities much closer together. The urgency of now is amplified by the global student demographic in large urban cities and the perennial gap between teachers and school leaders who come from the communities they serve. Global Majorities are no longer ethnic minorities, visible minorities or people of colour juxtaposed against white norms; people of the Global Majority are the norm. This chapter reflects on how culturally literate leadership draws heavily on scholarly work such as culturally responsive and sensitive leadership. It also explores how Black and Asian leaders need to shift out of a minority mindset and play a leading role in co-creating a new ecosystem between home and school.

**Keywords** Culturally literate • Culturally competent • Educational leadership • Culturally responsive

© The Author(s), under exclusive license to Springer Nature Switzerland AG 2021
R. M. Campbell-Stephens, *Educational Leadership and the Global Majority*, https://doi.org/10.1007/978-3-030-88282-2_5

Today the pernicious and dehumanising impact of systemic, institutionalised and structural anti-Black racism is exposed across the globe and at every level of education. From the morally incomprehensible expulsions of three-year-old children from pre-schools in the USA (Kirp, 2021; Gilliam & Reyes, 2016) and the UK to the refusal to award tenure to award-winning Black academics in top universities (Matthew, 2016), the hubristic contempt for Black humankind is clear for all to see. Racial inequity, inferiorisation, minoritisation and subordination are baked into our education systems. Some manifestations are insidious, such as Black students falling between the two stools of standardised testing, one rooted in eugenicists theory (Brigham, 1923) or the other teachers' assessment being riddled with unconscious bias (Burgess & Greaves, 2009). Either way, the Black and sometimes Brown child is labelled as underachieving compared with their peers. In other ways the system is overt, with Black boys labelled deviant and being four times as likely to be excluded from school as their white counterparts (Gillborn et al., 2016) or Asian, African and Caribbean overseas trained teachers (Miller & Callender, 2019) having to face punitive, humiliating and cruel additional requirements to achieve qualified teacher status compared with their white counterparts from Canada, the USA, Australia or New Zealand. The demographic shifts in our cities now make this level of systemic, structural racism, whether covert or overt, morally, ethically or economically unsustainable.

London school census data from January 2021 indicates that 73.2 per cent of pupils in London schools are from ethnic minority groups. If Black lives truly matter, then we need culturally literate, responsive and sensitive anti-racist leadership in our schools, because the impact of the status quo currently is that Black lives do not matter. When anti-Black racism is seriously addressed, everyone benefits. But, can a system that once used the same methods of calculating increase, decrease, purchase, sale, death, appreciation and depreciation for Black people as they did for livestock, ever truly value Black lives? An explicit intentional focus on deconstructing and eradicating systemic racism has to be an essential requirement in leadership, but this will present a real challenge in the present political context and policy environment following the publication of the controversial Commission on Race and Ethnic Disparities (2021) in the UK, for example, which was universally condemned including by the United Nations, for opinions such as the following:

[G]eography, family influence, socio-economic background, culture and religion have more significant impact on life chances than the existence of racism.' Among other things, the report blames single parents for poor outcomes, ignoring the racial disparities and the racialised nature of poor outcomes that exist despite an increased prevalence of single-parent families in every demographic. The report's conclusion that racism is either a product of the imagination of people of African descent or of discrete, individualised incidents ignores the pervasive role that the social construction of race was designed to play in society, particularly in normalising atrocity, in which the British state and institutions played a significant role.

Stunningly, the report also claims that, while there might be overt acts of racism in the UK, there is no institutional racism. The report offers no evidence for this claim, but openly blames identity politics, disparages complex analyses of race and ethnicity using qualitative and quantitative research, proffers shocking misstatements and/or misunderstandings about data collection and mixed methods research, cites 'pessimism', 'linguistic inflation', and 'emotion' as bases to distrust data and narratives associated with racism and racial discrimination, and attempts to delegitimise data grounded in lived experience while also shifting the blame for the impacts of racism to the people most impacted by it. (Statement by independent UN experts, April 2021)

Contemporary political contexts and events in 2021 therefore make it even more difficult to address systemic and institutionalised racism when there is vehement denial at state level of its very existence. The real contexts in which diverse communities live are significantly affected by systemic forms of discrimination on a daily basis. So, leaders understanding these realities have to deftly manoeuvre within their spheres of influence, the school within the community. As schools within urban contexts become more diverse, there are aspects of that context that cannot be ignored, especially when the student demographic live racialised lives. For many the impact of racialisation, systemic racism and white supremacy presents a greater threat than the coronavirus. Where there is a resistance among practitioners and policymakers alike, to acknowledge the differential impact of their practice on different groups, they become part of the problem rather than the solution. In the recent past, adopting a colour-blind approach meant either ignoring the significance of context, or, in contrast, problematising that context by burying notions of race within the code of 'disadvantage' or the rhetoric of inclusion. Now, in addition, ignoring the impact of structural racism is a matter of life and death.

The concept of co-production is not common within education and is primarily referred to in the literature as an example of direct user involvement in the production of services, more routinely in the areas of urban regeneration, housing, healthcare and social care. However, co-production of educational provision could, in the current context of reimagining education, provide a shift infrequently explored in the co-production literature. For researchers, this means shifting attention away from the individual leader towards processes of co-production that cultivate and develop leaders at all levels of the system. A co-production perspective provides leaders themselves with a deeper understanding of what it means to lead and also gives them an opportunity to reflect on what constitutes leadership activities. In addition, it begs the important questions: on whose authority do we lead and in whose interests? Co-production does require a predisposition and the requisite training to facilitate participation from marginalised and minoritised sections of society, as well as a redefining of traditional roles that is inclusive.

Co-production is enhanced when the perspective of communities served is not just acknowledged as 'community knowledge' but is central to the professional knowledge brought to bear in diverse contexts. Co-production, in the new normal where schools do not have a monopoly on organised learning, takes on new meaning. Co-production from a worldview must honestly interrogate the impact of inequitable educational provision on generations of the current majorities in our classrooms and communities. As co-production relies on professionals and service users producing together, this chapter will explore how the process works when significant numbers of the service users are from ethnically, linguistically and culturally diverse backgrounds and traditional imbalances of power and hierarchies of knowledge remain.

Reimagining education and school systems in a Covid world where Black lives *do* matter presents new opportunities to displace deficit thinking as well as the obvious challenges. Black Lives Matter and Covid-19 have laid bare the inequities in our societies, requiring systemic decolonial change, in every aspect of life. While there may be little consensus among the stakeholders about what education should look like going forward, there is growing consensus among the Global Majority about what it should not look like (Lopez, 2020). Leadership within the sector should be prefaced on truth, trust, consent and collaboration with communities directly impacted by the schools with which they are partnering. Given the current global reckoning with race, there must be a specific focus on race inequity within education, acknowledging the virulent strain of anti-Black racism that has now been unleashed on those minoritised Black within society. With the fastest-growing demographic in our schools being students from the Global Majority, these inequities are not sustainable—continuing a colour-blind approach to education is no more an option than a race-blind approach to Covid-19. The disproportionate impacts of both on Black and other minoritised communities cannot be ignored in the urgency of now. It is both a moral and an ethical issue.

There are some bold conversations to be had about educational purpose that will lead to fundamental questions about how we now need our education systems to function. Clichéd phrases like 'regardless of race, gender, income level, socio-economic level or location' should be replaced with 'with due regard to race, gender, income level, socio-economic or location'. We need to humanise our systems to see us, in our intersectional entirety, understanding how the intersections of race, gender, disability and socio-economic status impact lives. Reimagining therefore begins with reimagining purpose. It requires a new way of critiquing what is and unlearning, accepting that schools are now part of a learning ecosystem and that a new form of co-creation is required to meet new responsibilities. From a Global Majority perspective, I do not believe that schools in major cities across the globe realise that those groups previously racialised as minorities are actually the Global Majority. The education systems that need to be reimagined need to be reimagined from the perspective of the majority. These are matters not just for major cities in the Western world, but in former colonies. Will the current form of their education systems fit their new global status given the emergence of a new world order?

Of course, these are not new considerations. As Brown (2005) observed,

> '[S]chools in a racially diverse society will require leaders and models of leadership that will address the racial, cultural, and ethnic makeup of the school community'. However, while researchers during the past several decades have begun to investigate and interrogate the complicated dynamics of race and school leadership (e.g., Bryant 1998; Dantley & Tillman, 2006; Lopez, 2020; Tillman 2002), these issues remain among the largest elephants in the schoolhouse about which few practitioners or scholars will speak (Brooks & Gaetane, 2007).

Acknowledging the cultural, ethnic, multi-linguistic and political contexts in which co-production in urban areas needs to take place is essential in a post-2020 world. Co-production, among other things, relies on adjustments to the constructs which inform professional identity and differentiate experts from lay people. So, how can it be enacted when (a) the lay people are from a range of cultural backgrounds and (b) some of these cultures are represented within the professional classes? It requires a profound change, incorporating cultural competence among the range of leadership attributes required to lead in diverse contexts.

Cultural literacy and culturally relevant pedagogy should form an integral but explicit part of leadership preparation programmes for educators, especially in culturally diverse urban contexts. It should not be taken for granted that culturally relevant leadership is a general disposition of leaders. In situations where the staff and leadership of schools are predominantly white and the student demographic consists of young people from the Global Majority, how can the Eurocentric hegemonic be renegotiated to make sense within the context? Also,

> If the teachers of the schools do not consider themselves to have a culture, then they cannot be expected to take into account the various cultures of the students sitting in their classrooms and adapt their instruction accordingly. (Fraise & Brooks, 2015)

This can leave already marginalised students further disadvantaged, as while schools may talk about inclusion and diversity, this still assumes a white norm into which diversity will be included by being absorbed. As laudable as having better representation at senior leadership levels is, unless a new space is created for diverse leaders and those leaders leading in diverse contexts to develop epistemologies that actually lead to different leadership practices and organisational cultures, their presence will make no difference. Leadership preparation has to encourage both the diversification of those engaged in leadership and the models of leadership they develop. Culturally relevant pedagogy and racially literate leadership have much to offer in this regard.

However, there are other forms of leadership that value, even celebrate, culture, and build schooling around it rather than seek to change it. This is at the heart of an approach to education called 'culturally relevant pedagogy', an orientation toward schooling articulated and explored initially by Ladson-Billings and her colleagues over several decades of sustained conceptual and empirical inquiry (Ladson-Billings 1992, 1995a, 1995b, 1995c, 1997, 1998). Schools should foster a culture that takes all cultures into account with their formal and informal curricula and policies. This type of school atmosphere provides an environment in which students feel safe enough to be themselves and in which their anxiety is lowered to the point where they can concentrate on learning in a culturally safe environment. Culturally relevant pedagogy allows them to learn in the manner that best fits them, and it emphasises several propositions that ask educators to think about and practice their work a bit differently than is typically the case (Delpit, 1995).

Therefore, the five key themes explored in this chapter are as follows:

- What does it mean to be culturally literate leaders of culturally competent schools?
- Why does being culturally literate matter for leaders in schools?
- What are some of the challenges to co-production in diverse contexts?
- Is interrupting and changing the prevailing deficit narrative around those communities most vulnerable to underachievement and disengagement within the education system important to building community resilience?
- What are the implications for leadership preparation programmes to be culturally responsive, moving from a minority to a majority mindset?

The purpose of the chapter is building theory and practice through exploration of the five themes, as there is a paucity of research in the UK educational context about the dynamics of ethnicity, racial diversity, culture and school leadership in a systemically racist system. The attitude of school leaders to the communities they serve will set the parameters for the extent to which true co-production can take place. This chapter contextualises the leadership philosophy promoted in the Investing in Diversity (IiD) (Campbell-Stephens, 2009) leadership preparation programme in the light of London demographics and continuing under-representation of Black leaders in the school and college sector, even in 2021. I will avoid describing in depth the aims of the IiD programme or provide examples of the curriculum as this has been done elsewhere (Coleman & Campbell-Stephens, 2010; Johnson & Campbell-Stephens, 2010). But I will make reference to one of the preliminary themes identified in the leadership philosophies, that of cultural literacy, and the high expectations of self and sense of responsibility for under-served student communities, that such kinds of leadership orientation are intended to inculcate. This will provide an alternative narrative on the process of schooling in diverse and urban contexts.

## What Does It Mean to Be Culturally Literate?

Being culturally literate is essentially being able to understand the role of culture in human relationships and how organisations work. For the individual it is about understanding first and foremost one's own culture. Coming to terms with your roots and understanding how it underpins the way in which you think and make sense of meaning are crucial leadership attributes, especially, though not exclusively, in diverse contexts. Understanding one's own culture is a prerequisite to beginning to understand others, and what happens when different cultures collide. Those we serve, as well as those we lead, are at least partially culturally defined, as are the organisations and communities in which we all live and work (Arvizu & Savariia-Shore, 1990).

I have chosen the term 'culturally literate' instead of 'culturally competent' to explore the concept as something more deeply embedded and organic than acquisition through training of a set of skills, or the ability to perform certain tasks, as can be inferred by the use of the word 'competence'. I do, however, accept that in certain disciplines, such as social work, or in certain contexts such as the USA, the term 'culturally competent' is often applied to organisations, systems and individuals. On the Black and Asian Leadership Initiative (BALI) for aspiring Directors of Children's Services run by the Staff College in the UK, the cultural competence continuum, adapted by Meera Spillett (2018) from Terry L. Cross (1998) and Juli Coffin (2007), is used to identify the stages of cultural competence at which organisations might find themselves at any given time. Participants find the model adds significant depth to their understanding about how organisations' practices intersect with culture. The six stages are as follows:

- Cultural destructiveness
- Cultural incapacity
- Cultural blindness

- Cultural pre-competence
- Cultural competence
- Cultural proficiency

Some commentators in the USA refer to cultural sensitivity or global competency, each of which has similar characteristics to cultural literacy and cultural competence. In the UK there has been some work in the territory of providing culturally sensitive or appropriate service provision, particularly, but not exclusively, in the health sector. Being culturally literate is a way of being and seeing, which includes being culturally aware and intelligent; it is a state of mind that provides a lens through which you can read, view and experience the world. It is therefore a way of being and says much more about who you are than what you actually do. Co-production requires 'clients' to be seen as capable, responsible, situated, active participants in creating their own lives. In the education sector, those communities that have traditionally been failed by the system are not ordinarily seen as the protagonist, but rather as the spectator or victim. This narrative can now be intentionally and permanently disrupted by the right kind of leadership.

## Operationalising Cultural Literacy

An operational definition of cultural literacy is that of a globally competent person with enough substantive knowledge, perceptual understanding and intercultural communication skills to effectively interact in our globally interdependent world. In the case of a globally competent organisation, there are both a sufficient number of people who have this knowledge, understanding and skills as well as a culture that promotes such competency. There are essentially four components to being culturally competent: (a) awareness of one's own cultural worldview, (b) attitude towards cultural differences, (c) knowledge of different cultural practices and worldviews, and (d) cross-cultural skills.

Much is made of the importance of educators being able to empower students to become contributing citizens of an interdependent global village. Educators certainly need to be able to navigate that terrain with ease for themselves if this aspect of education is to be realised for them, their students, colleagues and the organisational culture. The PISA 2018 Global Competence assessment measures for students, for example, help in this regard as they offer much by way of identifying the skills, knowledge, values and attitudes that educators working through a Global Majority prism need. The competences include: the capacity to examine local, global and intercultural issues; understanding and appreciating the perspectives and worldviews of others; engaging in open appropriate and effective interactions across cultures; and taking action for collective well-being and sustainable development.

Local Authorities or, increasingly, networks of schools, including Multi-Academy Trusts (MATs) in places like the UK, must work in respectful partnerships with the communities they serve to reimagine and co-produce a culturally appropriate and sensitive educational offer. Therefore, ease with and appreciation of the role of culture, diversity and the challenges posed through long-standing inequity and differential power relations is a pre-requisite for leadership.

The explicit approach that was developed to providing culturally literate leadership preparation in the Investing in Diversity programme took three forms. The first was in the selection of tutors, who were in the main from a Black, Asian or other 'minority ethnic' background, or were colleagues from 'non-minoritised' backgrounds who worked successfully in diverse contexts. The second was through the programme content, in which each module was addressed from a critical race perspective. The third was through the approach to learning employed, where participants were encouraged to develop a professional identity that acknowledged their additionality, by virtue of their cultural background, which was valued and foregrounded through the programme as an essential asset. This kind of ongoing professional development is needed in order for educators to confidently and effectively educate students for an interconnected world. It is also important that a space is created, intellectually and otherwise, for educators from diverse backgrounds to not only rise through the ranks of the education system but to influence the processes and structures of that system, so that they are more equitable, affirming and inclusive of us all. In order for this to happen there need to be strong connected communities of practice that are intergenerational and that pass on knowledge, mentor, coach and are proactive in succession planning for the next generation of leaders. Key to developing these communities of practice is bespoke leadership development that centres the decolonising of the cognitive process that sets limiting beliefs in the minds of those racialised as minorities. In order for the education system to catch up with the facts that a system whose impact, intentional or not, has served to underserve the minorities that are now the majority in urban contexts, it has to radically change. It is my contention that new leadership paradigms, global wisdom and different lenses are needed to navigate the current spaces and challenges that we face, while maximising the opportunities to innovate.

## Why Does It Matter How Culturally Literate You Are as a Leader in Education?

A culturally literate person is likely to be comfortable with who they are, while still learning and being open to change. They will have come to terms with their roots, having invested time in coming to know themselves in their multifaceted lives. This leaves them open to and interested in diversity and others—open to, not threatened, concerned, in competition with or overwhelmed by. Teams of culturally literate people are more likely to be of a distributed leadership predisposition, and are better able to build culturally competent organisations, with leadership at all levels.

There is much educational research literature on leadership, and extensive writing on the under-representation of Black and other minority ethnic school leaders in the UK. There is a paucity of research within the British context that examines explicitly the relationship between the culture of the leader, how leadership is enacted and the epistemologies that are emerging of Black and Asian school leaders—if, as my observations over some forty years have led me to believe, and my work on the Investing in Diversity programme with over 1000 aspiring leaders confirmed, we bring who we are to what we do. Who we are as leaders is at least as important as what we do as leaders, and therefore the act of leadership cannot be a neutral activity, because we are not neutral (Portelli & Campbell-Stephens, 2009).

Principals', and in the UK, CEOs of MATs, understanding and skills pertaining to diversity are important in leading diverse schools and preparing all students for a more democratic and multi-cultural society. Although educational leadership scholars have theorised about exemplary leadership of and for diversity, a developmental perspective on principals' diversity or cultural competence remains absent (Hernandez & Kose, 2012). Leadership preparation as traditionally conceived takes the opposite view and tends to treat leaders as a homogenous group where what they do matters more than who they are relying on the perception that leadership theories, practices and curricula are neutral and free of cultural perspectives and beliefs, according to Lumby and Morrison (2010). 'Neutral' and

94 R. M. CAMPBELL-STEPHENS

'free of cultural perspectives' can also be code for 'white', Western epistemologies of knowledge taken as the norm, outside of which educators of colour, sit, waiting or alongside their communities pleading to be seen, heard and included.

Research has confirmed that an important aspect of leading for equity, embracing diversity and striving for social justice, involves diversity self-awareness and self-reflection. This includes facilitating faculty discussions on privilege, inequities, racism and raising expectations for all students, and advocating for and understanding the backgrounds of traditionally marginalised students (DeMatthews & Mawhinney, 2014; Dantley & Tillman, 2006; Kose, 2007; Theoharis, 2007).

Individuals as well as organisations have culture, a set of values and beliefs by which they operate, subversively and sometimes overtly. The predominating culture can determine the purpose of individuals if they are not secure in their own purpose as human beings. The same is true of organisations and how they go about their daily business. If the predominating school culture is contemptuous, dismissive, paternal or patronising of the cultures of the students they serve, the behaviour of the organisation will epitomise this. Understanding and appreciation of 'the other' are essential for true co-production and respectful engagement to take place. A predisposition, therefore, towards cultural literacy is particularly important for school leaders who serve diverse communities, in the same way that a doctor, however well-qualified, needs to understand the context of their patients' lived reality, including their beliefs, customs and practices, in order that they can provide effective and appropriate medical care.

A headteacher, deemed to be outstanding, who led a primary school in an urban setting outside of London in the UK, on being asked during a training session by another school leader what sort of activities her young largely Asian students of Pakistani heritage, were engaged in during their summer holidays, blithely replied, 'Nothing. These children do nothing in their holidays.. We had just spent the morning speaking to some of the brightest, most articulate, funny Year 5 children that I have had the pleasure to meet, falling over themselves to tell us their visitors about what they had been doing in school that term. It was evident from the answers that we received from our little group that most of the children had some foundation language skills in at least two languages other than English and were very proud of this. Yet this outstanding head, and she was in many respects just that, leading a training session for other headteacher colleagues about leading in diverse contexts, felt that her students did nothing at home during the summer which contributed to the students' excellent academic results during term time. Incredulous that such a stereotype would go unchallenged, especially as there were some Asian school leaders present, I sat silently, but eavesdropped on the murmurings among some of those same leaders as they talked among themselves during the coffee break. Massive elephants in the room—if this white leader had such a deficit model in her head about the home environments in which those children lived and felt at ease to share them in a training session where she was the cultural minority, one can only imagine how conversations went when she was just among white colleagues. Now in a post Covid-19 world where good schools will be co-creating with parents and students new ways of learning, how can this be accomplished where there is such arrogance, white racism and deficit thinking on the part of the school and its leadership?

Contrast this with the young African Caribbean early years manager in the same city who also trains staff to work in diverse preschool contexts in a way that acknowledges that the communities that they serve have knowledge. She described her children as entering the early years settings 'with a rich and individual catalogue of experiences that have all contributed to their own personal narratives'. In one of her training sessions she demonstrates skilfully, through the retelling of a real story, how to use a three-year-old's retelling of what he did over the weekend to (a) affirm his identity, (b) develop his confidence, (c) build racial affinity and build on the learning experience, as she too had seen the same film that he was so excited about, and (d) begin to challenge some of the sexist thoughts that he was beginning to have about different characters and roles. This teacher leader used an excited little boy's 'burst of words, with great uses of adjectives and expression, clear intonation and pauses' to not just teach, but learn, about his family, his culture, who and what is important to him and his passion for role play. Even the use of the expression 'burst of words' conveys the passion, energy and love for her student (Pemberton, 2020).

## What Are Some of the Challenges to Leading and Co-constructing in Current Diverse Contexts?

At the time of writing, 2021, deep structural race inequity in Britain, the USA and across the globe is undeniable. Anti-Black racism has been laid bare in every institution and aspect of life. Yet the aggressive push back from the white establishment is such that calling out racism is deemed more offensive than racism itself. There is an openly hostile state-sanctioned environment to equity and social justice based on race. The racial contract remains unbroken, anchored in white supremacy at a time when the fastest growing demographic in major cities are young people of the Global Majority. This is challenging territory for the anti-racist school leader. It requires a radical re-think about educational purpose.

> An ethical and democratic globality, and the kind of education that would contribute to it, are only possible in the context of a recognition of the relations of power that have shaped history, and in particular the political, cultural, economic and epistemological processes of domination that have characterised colonialism and Eurocentrism (De Lissovoy, 2010).

In the midst of current systems imploding, a massive opportunity is emerging. A radically new vision for globalisation is needed, one in which the Global Majority which constitutes eight-five per cent of the world's population sees itself reflected. The existing political and economic globalisation process delivering current levels of imbalance and inequity is unsustainable. In 2006 the director of the Division for the Promotion of Quality Education stressed the importance of the work of UNESCO in addressing today's challenges of globalisation and cultural diversity, as well as the increasing demands from member states for information on the role of education in building dynamic and versatile societies that are respectful of cultural differences. In 2021, historical epistemologies based on racialisation, colonisation and domination through cultural erasure and subordination will be insufficient to the scale of reimagining required.

At a local level in places such as England, ambitious co-production within diverse contexts must acknowledge that the activity is bound by context. It cannot pretend that racialised diversity does not exist within that context, or that the relationship between the state and all of its citizens is the same. For example, many members of immigrant communities under the Hostile Environment policy, and Asian Muslim young people under the Prevent Strategy do not feel a sense of belonging, but a sense of being a threat while being under surveillance. Schools serving these communities have to understand and engage with the realities of that kind of oppressive, stressful and 'othering' existence. It is a disturbing default position for a school system serving increasingly varied diversity when that diversity is positioned as a threat to the wider society. Organisations and those that lead them are deemed to be neutral, when clearly they are not. Diversity, where acknowledged at all is too often conceived of in these contexts as a deficit, problematic, challenging, something to deny, ignore, be defensive or apologetic or even get angry about. Within Western education systems serving diverse communities, being multi-lingual, coming from certain faith groups, or being Black, is often synonymous with challenge, deprivation or worst still, something threatening to the prevailing culture. The groups themselves are seen to be the problem, to have failed to assimilate, to have deviant values, to be inferior culturally, to have poor parental or community support and not to value education as 'we' know it. The notion of co-production where there is such a hierarchy of power, values and agency, where what one set of partners brings to the table is deemed to be so much less than others, simply reinforces the status quo. Diversity through this lens is not viewed as adding any value and is more likely to be seen as synonymous with failure and disengagement and a drain on scarce resources. The failure is rarely viewed as systemic, but always the failure of either the 'disengaged' who pose the 'difference' and those who would act in their interest. A clear example of systemic failure to embrace difference is the way in which initial teacher training, or indeed professional development at any stage throughout an educator's career in cities such as London, reflects explicitly the pedagogical developments and skills needed to teach in diverse contexts such as London.

In a city where upwards of 300 different languages are spoken and seventy-five per cent of the student demographic are from 'ethnic minority' Global Majority communities, this fact is not reflected in the training that teachers in London receive. Yet if a student teacher were training at Shortwood Teachers Training College in Kingston, Jamaica for example, part of that training would include conversational Spanish, because of the accepted importance of Spanish in that region of the world. Some would argue, somewhat lamely, given the above example, that there are too many languages represented in London's schools and colleges for one or two to be selected for teacher training. But even when the system was dealing with far fewer languages 30 years ago, the policy of assimilation within the education system ensured that no real thought was given to the fact that cities like London would continue to become more diverse, not less, over the decades to come, and that the British system of teacher training and later leadership preparation might need to adapt to accommodate this. It was assumed that all of this diversity would be assimilated to the point of oblivion. And besides, English is a universal language.

## THE IMPORTANCE OF CHANGING PREVAILING DEFICIT NARRATIVES AROUND SOME COMMUNITIES

A decolonial global orientation towards school leadership will critique school curricula, processes, practices and policies that fail such significant proportions of the student body. The system's incapacity to accommodate difference without problematising it has led to some 'received wisdoms' about diverse contexts. A fundamental systemic and cultural change is needed, led by an alternative narrative, a lens trained on the system itself and accompanying policy scrutiny as they affect those groups that have traditionally been failed by our education systems.

More often than not there is a discourse of deficit surrounding those groups that are described as disadvantaged and which tend to be Black or other Global Majority students, as well as white students who come from poor socio-economic backgrounds. Cynically, the system, now that it is denying institutionalised racism and changing the way that it collects data, is pitting Black students against white working-class students to whom government departments now say they want to shift the equity focus. Too often, the students, their parents and their backgrounds are viewed as problems to be fixed. These groups might not naturally be seen as rich resources in any co-producing activity. While accepting that social, political, economic and cultural factors all have an impact on levels and pace of achievement, some of the inequity is deeply systemic, led by leaders without efficacy. Morally centred, equity-focused, culturally responsive leadership can and always does significantly ameliorate the worst excesses of any system and open doors for the people they serve to be the empowered authors of their lives, rather than the spectators of their wretchedness.

Regrettably, too many teacher educators are no more capable than their counterparts were thirty or forty years ago to provide professional development for teachers that properly equips them to work effectively as transformational educators in diverse urban settings. Instead, the urban landscape continues to be perceived as challenging for educators, one in which only the exceptional teacher or leader can make a difference. The blame for academic underachievement is laid firmly at the door of poor parenting, youth culture, poverty, the media, the backgrounds of students, society, in fact anywhere but within the sphere of influence of the school, the quality of teaching, and the leadership thereof. Co-production in this context must take place in a newly created space, where schools and the communities they serve come together to provide appropriate and sustainable service provision. They may have to look to examples outside of education, like the world of business and commerce, where diversity is seen as an asset.

In their study of successful urban superintendents, Skrla and Scheurich (2001) explain that many (particularly white) teachers, principals and superintendents, 'tend to view the broad-scale under-performance of children of color and children from low-income homes in their schools as inevitable, something that is not within their power to change'. We in the UK were not helped by headlines such as 'Genetics outweighs teaching' (Cummings, 2013), when describing the challenge that schools serving largely white working-class communities face. Government funding for the Sure Start area-based initiative was soon cut following the release of the government's adviser's unpublished but highly influential paper, 'Genetics outweighs teaching', the title of which speaks clearly for itself. Launched in 1998 by Tessa Jowell MP, Sure Start had similarities to the much older, and similarly named, Head Start programme in the USA and is also comparable to Australia's Head Start and Ontario's Early Years Plan. The initiatives were subsequently bound together to form Sure Start Children's Centres, and responsibility for them was transferred to local government. Tessa Jowell commented in 2015, 'I am very proud of setting up Sure Start, because the first three years of a child's life are absolutely critical in determining the chances they have subsequently'. This kind of defunding of equity-based initiatives poses huge problems, particularly in a recession, for an education system where the fastest growing groups in urban areas are from underachieving groups where their teachers and teacher leaders really feel that they are powerless to change the inevitable. If teachers look at their class of students and can only see poor socio-economic and ethnic backgrounds, a class full of stereotypes that are beyond their ability to influence, then schools and the process of schooling are reduced to control and containment facilities. With the instances of certain private companies running both local education services and provision for the criminal justice system, you can see why some communities are very worried. The UK government has just in 2021 allocated the first tranche of money, ten million pounds, to its behaviour hub programme, its latest initiative, while cutting all funding to diversifying leadership in schools.

Historically, advocacy by Black parents and community members has been critical in the development of Britain's equity policies and programmes, particularly in places like London and Birmingham. Against such a context, leadership preparation cannot afford to be either colour blind or ignore its legacy. In fact, co-production should find fertile territory in places such as the London boroughs of Hackney, Haringey, Lewisham, Newham, Tower Hamlets, Waltham Forest and Wandsworth, UK cities like Birmingham, Bristol, Leeds Manchester, and due to the deep, strong and long legacy of community activism and culture of self-help.

Truly, outstanding and visionary leaders perceive leadership very differently in these contexts; they feel privileged to provide leadership in the communities they serve and reject utterly the disadvantage narrative. The diversity is what makes the role worthwhile and from which they draw strength. They are much more likely to view the role of educator as a vocation than a job, or career step. They see it as their role to not only understand those communities but to be vociferous advocates for them and build capacity for them to advocate for themselves. They build sufficient moral authority so that when they have to challenge those same communities, they are on safe ground to do so, because of their investment in developing trust and respect. They make a difference with students that might otherwise (and certainly in other schools) have fallen over the precipice; they are efficacious because they have chosen to be so and believe in their purpose. In addition, given that most urban areas are significantly multi-cultural, to adopt a so-called 'post racial' narrative is to ignore one of the great elephants in the room, that of race. How can we change the prevailing narrative if you can't even talk about the issues?

There is a real reluctance, fatigue or sometimes open hostility now to address issues of race in an education system that stubbornly rejects claims of institutionalised racism or discrimination in the face of overwhelming evidence to the contrary. Apparently, even while African Caribbean boys, generations after their great grandparents settled in the UK, still remain four times as likely to be excluded from school, or be educated in alternative provision, in either case remaining vulnerable to significant underachievement, we as educators do not need to have an explicit focus on this. We don't need to act on our own research that tells us that school inspections fail to report disproportionate exclusions of Black students, even though some of those inspection reports include the statistics that clearly demonstrate that this is the case. Social disadvantage, measured by free school meals, which have become the proxy for 'white working class', is now the only equity issue that can be discussed, without people feeling threatened, and even then, it is a deliberately dishonest and dividing discourse.

Runnymede's research on race and class prejudice, alongside our work on educational outcomes for BME students, has found that positioning white working-class disadvantage as an ethnic disadvantage rather than as class disadvantage places this group in direct competition with minority ethnic groups, and does very little to address the real and legitimate grievances of poor white people in Britain. The plight of these white children is a class issue rather than a race issue and this is an important distinction. Their discrimination takes place because of their class, not because of their whiteness (Treloar, 2021).

This is morally detrimental to the development of a cohesive and equitable society.

The same is true in the USA, where in one study it was found that

> Black school leaders and white school leaders engaged, apparently by mutual consent, in a 'conspiracy of silence' and refrained from acknowledging, discussing, or engaging issues of race with each other. White school leaders tended to dismiss issues of race as issues of class, while Black school leaders refrained from discussing issues of race with their white colleagues, since they saw no safe forum in which they could broach the subject. White school leaders' strategy of shifting the topic from race to class enabled them to avoid uncomfortable conversations with each other and with their Black colleagues. White leaders commonly explained, as did this teacher, that a few examples here and there were evidence that class, and not race, was the operational issue:

> I know this one African American kid whose father is a doctor and mother is a lawyer. The kid drives a nicer car than I do, and he speaks perfect English, not all that ghetto slang. He does great in school. So, I think it's more about coming from a family that doesn't have those ghetto values. It isn't about race, it's about class. (Brooks & Gaetane, 2007)

Now with the attacks on epistemic lenses such as Critical Race Theory gaining such prominence, the concerns are that these pushbacks on race equality are to silence those voices who are challenging school curricula that are Eurocentric, have colonial roots and are resistant to addressing systemic racism in our history and current-day society in an honest and balanced way. The weaponising of the white working-class narrative is deliberate; the conspiracy of silence around race is also deliberate, and while in some limited cases may be about discomfort in talking about race, is much more likely to be about not caring enough about race to be honest about what is going on.

## THE IMPLICATIONS FOR LEADERSHIP
## PREPARATION PROGRAMMES

A Eurocentric, colour-blind, colonial approach to educational leadership development, where 'legitimate knowledge' shuts out the diversity that the system claims it seeks and precludes inclusion of those who bring other epistemological and ontological approaches to leadership, is also deliberate. This results in the needs of those racialised and minoritised communities who constitute the Global Majority, and on whom urban economies increasingly rely, to be deemed not of worthy of prioritisation within those systems to warrant acknowledgement or change.

There is a need to understand the political context nationally and globally and how this is impacting the lives of the communities that we serve as well as our lives. On the weekend of 11 July 2021, the Euro 2020 football final was held at Wembley Stadium in London. (Euro 2020 took place in 2021, as due to the Coronavirus the tournament was postponed in 2020.) The final was between England and Italy and it was decided by a penalty shootout which Italy won, 3–2. Three of the penalty takers for the English team were Black, one of them only 19, and because they missed their penalties, they were subject to the vilest of racist abuse and threats, including death threats, on social media. Black parents and no doubt conscious Black teachers were on the alert for the backlash against young Black men and boys in London and elsewhere that would take place on the streets the morning after the match. There were incidents of young men and school children on their way to school the next day, who were physically beaten and verbally abused, as 'niggers' and 'monkeys' because they 'looked like' any one of the three footballers, or indeed just because they were Black. This is the reality of being racialised Black in England in 2021, where parents and teachers will have to be providing guidance to young Black men and children about not being out on the streets and how to stay safe if they have to go out, including to school. This is how precarious Black lives are in a city like London in 2021. Those students and parents in London need to know that leadership preparation for their school principals is at the very least cognisant of the lived reality of being racialised Black, especially when the official government line is that Britain is not structurally and systemically racist.

The colonial roots of the education systems that we are a product of have to be acknowledged and understood by educators because racial inequity continues to be a problem in every aspect of life for Black and Asian people. Efforts to recruit new teachers from BAME groups are important but these alone will not solve shortages. Nationally, retention is lower for BAME teachers than for white British teachers (Allen et al. 2016; DfE 2018c). Scholars and commentators often employ 'a revolving door' metaphor to emphasise the problems of high turnover (i.e., moving schools) and high attrition (i.e. leaving the profession) of new teachers, both of which are particularly prevalent in schools in deprived areas (Allen et al., 2018). An approach focused on understanding the causes of minority teacher staffing problems in relation to institutional characteristics and the culture of the workplace has been useful to study the phenomenon (Ingersoll et al. 2019). Tereshchenko et al. (2021) Leadership preparation cannot afford to be colour-blind, and racial literacy has to be an essential criterion for leadership in diverse urban contexts, especially as the lack of it among the senior leadership team is one of the key reasons for the attrition rate of early-career BAME teachers.

> This 'colour-blind' approach (Mabokela and Madsen 2003) to leadership development, where leadership theories, practices, and curriculum are thought to be neutral and free of cultural perspectives and beliefs, views aspiring school leaders as a 'homogeneous group where what they do matters more than who they are (Lumby & Morrison, 2010).

Headteachers and principals, CEOs, local authority advisers and others who support educational provision and school improvement should through their training better understand how the intersections of cultural, ethnic and racialised difference, educational practices, curricula, structures, assessment or institutionalised forms of discrimination precipitate and consolidate the persistent achievement gap between Black Caribbean and white students in the UK context. Ironically, if there is one community with which schools could successfully partner to co-produce anti-racist, decolonial, culturally appropriate, educational provision that would address decades-long inequalities in educational outcomes for Black Caribbean students, it is the Black Caribbean community. There is an extensive history of activism within the Black community in the field of education stemming back to Pan-African principles of self-determination and collective action on which co-production could build. Black supplementary schools, Black parent associations, Black teachers' sections and Black student sections within national unions, and the large base of Black scholarship creates unprecedented fertile territory to reimagine education focused on equity for a global demographic. It is a classic case that if we were to get it right for this community, with the disproportionate attainment rates, the over-representation in exclusions and the critical over-representation in the school-to-prison pipeline, we would have developed the building blocks to limit the worst excesses of the system on any vulnerable group, as we move to dismantling a structurally oppressive system for too many.

With the increased marketisation of education, there may be some lessons for the school sector to learn from the world of business and the health sector about the potential of embracing diversity, in the interest of being effective, enhancing quality, remaining relevant and improving sustainability. HSBC bank is recognised as a leading organisation for diversity and inclusion. HSBC acknowledges and celebrates its global roots and markets itself as the world's local bank, drawing heavily on local knowledge to do business, including having a connected workforce that reflects the communities where it operates. Through its advertisements, as well as through its organisational structures and ways of doing business, which include public commitments and actions, it demonstrates how important it is to understand the role of culture, and work with the set of values and beliefs that inform how different communities and societies operate. As an organisation in which diversity and inclusion are lead from the top, it provides a psychologically safe space for employees and proper support for wellbeing and career progression. There is substantive evidence in business that organisations benefit from more diversity in leaders and managers, for better decision-making, more creativity and better use of the potential of all employees, by investing in a wider talent pool, that keeps the business relevant. Can we afford to continue to problematise diversity in our school system instead of incorporating the benefits of diversity to make our society stronger and more progressive?

## CONCLUSION

Although Black and Asian educators have been leading British schools for over thirty years, their often unique, indigenous, self-defined leadership praxis and perspectives have received modest attention in the literature and have therefore not contributed to the theory-building and epistemologies of how to prepare successful school leaders. Where Black and Asian leaders' perspectives do feature in the literature, it is more generally to describe their under-representation. This may in part be true because of how the leaders themselves elect to identify, where they do not consider their ethnicity to be part of their professional or even personal identity. In contrast, perhaps, they were just never asked about how or whether their cultural identity and lived experiences contributed to the way they lead. There are some exceptions to this over the last fifteen years or so (Coleman & Campbell-Stephens, 2010; Johnson & Campbell-Stephens, 2010; Lumby & Morrison, 2010; Miller & Callender, 2019). Co-production can reframe this conversation.

In my extensive experience as an adviser for Institutional Review and Development for five years in a London borough essentially supporting headteachers and having developed and run leadership preparation programmes for a further thirteen years for the Institute of Education, University College London, and then for the National College for School Leadership, my practitioner research supports the argument that cultural backgrounds heavily influence leadership orientations, even if that influence for some Black and Asian leaders is to consciously adapt the dominant culture's leadership style, so as not to draw unwanted attention to their ethnicity. More often than not Black and Asian leaders developed the mantle of transformational leader and did so in contexts where their ethnicity and culture were highly valued aspects of additionality. They were also prepared to disrupt deficit narratives about communities from which many of them came or with which they identified.

In the National College for School Leaderships' campaign on succession planning, Bush (2011) notes that 'the diversity aspect has been the least successful' and that discourse about the need for more BME leaders is non-existent or marginalised in many local educational authorities (p. 191). What Bush failed to say is that the reason that the diversity aspect of the succession planning campaign was the least successful, however, that was being measured is that the diversity aspect of the succession planning work was oppositional to the coloniality of power within an impenetrable white system, and most importantly sat outside of government priorities. Britain remains systemically and structurally a deeply racist society, which has perpetrated the same detrimental effect across all sectors and all aspects of life for the majority of Black people.

Although many may disagree about the extent or degree of racism in Britain, there is no denying the growing disparities at societal levels in indicators of health, education, incarceration or inequity of opportunity and outcomes. Put differently, despite its espoused belief in equality (levelling the playing field for all) and equity (more for those who need it), the UK has created and reinforced a system of 'in-group' and 'out-group' along racial lines, producing, in effect, many nations within one nation, or enclaves, with their own experiences and their own internal and external racialised problems or privileges. Although much emphasis has been placed on the role of educational leaders in tackling racism in their institutions, it is also important to remember that educational institutions and educational leaders are by-products and microcosms of this overarching context—a context where inequity and inequality are endemic (Miller, 2020).

So, while bespoke leadership programmes can support underrepresented groups to first decolonise their minds of the limiting factors that, having been racialised and minoritised, many would have internalised; such programmes will be unable to shift 400 years of unbridled racism that dehumanised Black people, created a hierarchy of whiteness and white supremacy, with white men planted firmly at the top. That particular form of decolonisation in order to be 'effective', needs to be led by those who created it or at the very least those who benefit from and sustain it. But in order for that to happen, the hegemonic mind would have to see itself through the eyes of the other. As a former National College associate with responsibility for diversity and equality in 2011, my colleagues in that role and I were very much part of the 'out-group' that Miller refers to.

> This form of hegemonic 'consent' is the primary administrative mechanism of the 'racial contract' that Charles Mills describes as 'creat[ing] a universe of persons and sub persons' who are 'destined never to penetrate the normative rights ceiling established for them below white persons'. (Clennon, 2019)

It is from that vantage point, just under the ceiling, that I contend that on reflection, while some progress in programmes such as Investing in

Diversity in London achieved better representation of Black and Asian educators at leadership levels, the systemic barriers, while pushed were not crushed. What has not happened sufficiently at a systemic level, is the acceptance that to lead in diverse contexts, leaders require culturally competent and racially literate leadership preparation and a conducive political and policy context in which to operate. In today's openly racialised global environment I am reminded daily that the process of colonisation was not only violent, but took the form of ongoing denial, erasure and delusion, as well as dehumanisation for those who survived the violence. The colonial educational project was and remains a critical part of the neo-colonial's arsenal.

Settler colonialism invaded communities resulting in epistemic violence on indigenous and colonised people everywhere. This was done in part through education by destroying the ways of knowing and culture of those they colonised. The goal of colonisers and the colonising enterprise was to create homogenous understandings of social organising practices built around authority and leadership and centred the knowledge of the colonisers (Prakash and Esteva 2008). Garcia and Natividad (2018, p. 28) note that 'even though education is touted as social mobility and freedom for Indigenous peoples [including Indigenous peoples of Africa and other colonised spaces], the politics of knowledge production and dissemination are ultimately tied to modern Western ordering of the world' (Lopez, 2020).

A huge challenge remains in doing what really needs to be done, which is to decolonise education systems in both the former coloniser's countries as the youngest demographic of their major cities become the Global Majority and of course decolonise in the former colonies, as the current system has become redundant in either context.

Policymakers, some educators and their leaders may delude themselves that they live in a post-racial age, but in 2021 their students and the communities from which they come are under no such illusion, right across society, from the football terraces to the law courts, and the surveillance systems enroute, race and racialisation remain an issue in twenty-first-century Britain and across the globe.

## References

Arvizu, S., & Savariia-Shore, M. (1990). Cross-cultural literacy: An anthropological approach to dealing with diversity. *Education and Urban Society, 22*(4), 364–376.

Brigham, C. (1923). *A study of American intelligence. Kraus Reprint.* Millwood.

Brown, F. (2005). African Americans and school leadership: An introduction. *Educational Administration Quarterly, 41*(4), 585–590.

Brooks, J., & Gaetane, J. (2007). Black leadership, white leadership: Race and race relations in an urban high school. *Journal of Educational Administration, 45*(6), 756–768.

Burgess, S., & Greaves, E. (2009). *Test scores, subjective assessment and stereotyping of ethnic minorities.* University of Bristol. www.bristol.ac.uk/cmpo/publications/papers/2009/wp221.pdf

Bush, T. (2011). *Theories of educational leadership and management.* Sage Publications.

Campbell-Stephens, R. (2009). Investing in diversity: Changing the face (and the heart) of educational leadership. *School Leadership and Management, 29*(3), 321–331.

Clennon, O. (2019). *Black scholarly activism between the academy and grassroots: A bridge for identities and social justice.* Palgrave Macmillan.

Cummings, D. (2013). *Genetics outweighs teaching.* The Guardian

Coleman, M., & Campbell-Stephens, R. (2010). Perceptions of career progress: The experience of Black and minority ethnic school leaders. *School Leadership and Management, 30*(1), 35–49. https://doi.org/10.1080/13632430903509741

Commission on Race and Ethnic Disparities: The Report (2021).

Dantley, M. E., & Tillman, L. C. (2006). Social justice and moral transformative leadership. In C. Marshall & M. Oliva (Eds.), *Leadership for social justice: Making revolutions in education* (2nd ed., pp. 19–34). Allyn & Bacon.

De Lissovoy, N. (2010). Decolonial pedagogy and the ethics of the global. *Discourse: Studies in the Cultural Politics of Education, 31*(3), 279–293.

Delpit, L. (1995). *Other People's Children: Cultural Conflict in the Classroom.* New York Press.

DeMatthews, D., & Mawhinney, H. (2014). Social justice leadership and inclusion: Exploring challenges in an urban district struggling to address inequities. *Educational Administration Quarterly, 50*(5), 844–881.

Fraise, N., & Brooks, J. (2015). Toward a theory of culturally relevant leadership for school-community culture. *International Journal of Multicultural Education, 17*(1), 6–21. https://doi.org/10.18251/ijme.v17i1.983

Gillborn, D., Rollock, N., Warmington, P., & Demack, S. (2016). Race, racism and education: Inequality, resilience and reform in policy & practice. A two-year research project funded by the Society for Educational Studies (SES). National Award, 2013.

Gilliam, W. S., & Reyes, C. (2016). *Teacher decision-making factors that lead to preschool expulsion: Scale development and preliminary validation of the preschool expulsion risk measure.* Publisher?

Hernandez, F., & Kose, B. (2012). The Developmental Model of Intercultural Sensitivity: A Tool for Understanding Principals' Cultural Competence. *Education and Urban Society, 44*(4), 512–530.

Johnson, L., & Campbell-Stephens, R. (2010). Investing in diversity in London schools: Leadership preparation for black and global majority educators. *Urban Education, 45*, 480.

Kirp, D. (2021). A 4-year-old Child is not a problem. And expulsion is not a solution. There is an effective approach to breaking the preschool-to-prison pipeline. https://www.nytimes.com/2021/04/25/opinion/preschool-children-mental-health.html?smid=em-share

Kose, B. W. (2007). Principal leadership for social justice: Uncovering the content of teacher professional development. *Journal of School Leadership, 17*, 276–312.

Lopez, A. (2020). *Decolonizing educational leadership: Exploring alternative approaches to leading schools*. Palgrave Macmillan.

Lumby, J., & Morrison, M. (2010). Leadership and diversity: Theory and research. *School Leadership & Management, 30*(1), 3–17. https://doi.org/10.1080/13632430903509717

Matthew, P. (2016). *Written unwritten: Diversity and the hidden truths of tenure*. The University of North Carolina Press.

Miller, P., & Callender, C. (2019). *Race, education and educational leadership in England: An integrated analysis*. Bloomsbury Academic.

Pemberton, L. (2020). *Inclusion–'Wakanda forever'*. Nursery World.

Portelli, J., & Campbell-Stephens, R. (2009). *Leading for equity: The Investing in Diversity approach*. Edphil Books.

Skrla, L., & Scheurich, J. (2001). Displacing deficit thinking in school district leadership. *Education and Urban Society, 33*(3), 235–259.

Spillett, M. (2018). *Cultural competence: Promoting leadership & organisational change*. Staff College.

Tereshchenko, T., Mills, M., & Bradbury, A. (2021). *Making Progress? Employment and retention of BAME teachers in England*. Institute of Education.

Theoharis, G. (2007). Social justice educational leaders and resistance: Toward a theory of social justice leadership. *Educational Administration Quarterly, 43*, 221–258.

Treloar, N. (2021). The weaponisation of the 'left-behind white working class'. An article published in *Equality, Equalities Legislation, Politics*. The Runnymede Trust. Pages?

# CHAPTER 6

# Conclusion: Global Majority Back to the Future, a Possibility to Live Into

**Abstract** The chapter examines how leadership preparation models for progressive Global Majority leaders and indeed any school leaders serving an urban demographic could provide liberatory possibilities for us all to live into. Drawing on the work of Lopez (2020), where imagining and envisioning are described as central to educational theorising and practice, and are essential for decolonising educational leadership, I reflect on my journey of envisioning the Global Majority concept and how it may contribute to the scholarship on leadership and decoloniality in education and beyond. There are aspects of the concept that are still evolving, but exploration of more examples of the people of the Global Majority co-creating is beyond the scope of this book, such as Indigenous First Nation people of America, Canada, Australia and New Zealand. Paradigms of educational leadership that continue to relegate epistemologies and ways of being and seeing of the eighty-five per cent of the world's population to the margins of professional identity are not only breathtakingly hubristic but rob current and future generations of their opportunity through 'educere' to be the best version of themselves. The clock is ticking on a new globality.

**Keywords** Investing in Diversity self-determination • Decolonisation; Global Majority • Leadership preparation

© The Author(s), under exclusive license to Springer Nature
Switzerland AG 2021
R. M. Campbell-Stephens, *Educational Leadership and the Global Majority*, https://doi.org/10.1007/978-3-030-88282-2_6

On several webinars in the USA and Canada in which I have participated in recent months, the hosts have begun by recognising the original inhabitants of the land on which they currently stand. These acknowledgements of First Nation peoples' territory' on which we live and work at the very least show recognition and respect for the original inhabitants, some of whom within the Canadian and US contexts are still there. I have found this new convention both refreshing intellectually and moving spiritually; it feels distinctly non-white in approach, and familiar in African circles, where we acknowledge our ancestors also in a spirit of recognition and respect. I have looked forward to hearing new names and peoples that I have felt compelled to research afterwards. It sets a tone for those meetings that I find resonates deeply with me. It has struck me that connection to the land on which we stand and build and in which there is memory is something deeply primal, but it goes beyond this; there is a metaphor here of the past being layered rather than linear and therefore ever present. It speaks to acknowledging and telling the truth about that land's history, it's people and how we the current inhabitants got there. The personal irony of having built our retirement home on former plantation land has not escaped me. The former occupiers 'owners' of the land must be turning in their graves; literally, there is a grave next door of one such plantation owner who owned land and people (my ancestors) in this area. Our ancestors on the other hand must be dancing on their unmarked graves, as we them us, move from the plantation to the veranda and inside the house. At night sometimes, I feel them. It is from this perspective looking out at the Caribbean Sea, like the mythical African Sankofa bird, that I return to retrieve that which was lost in my culture and history to provide the scaffolding that leads to an agenda for the future.

The present historical moment demands of us a vision of globality that we can live into, where the world turns back to where it began to bring forward traditional values, that offers modernised life and new meaning to people everywhere. The transition to a new form of ethical and democratic globality represents a moment of opportunity to reimagine leadership preparation. A decolonising of leadership is only possible in the context of recognising the relations of power that has shaped what has taken place and remains in the layers of the land and the foundations of the institutions in which we serve. In particular, the racialisation and systematic dehumanisation have created epistemological processes of domination that have minoritised the Global Majority to ethnic minorities, erasing or silencing their authentic voice.

Very little is written in the western academies about the theories and practice of leadership and the dynamic that is created when western processes and models meet Black or other Global Majority cultures in the form of the leader. Leadership theory has for a long time been trapped in a white supremacist western mindset, with domestic theories masquerading as universal paradigms:

> Conceptualisations of leadership, paradigms of leadership theories and approaches are typically framed from a western mindset, very much consistent with a Eurocentric philosophy and ideology of a modern, globalised world that is dominated by the power and influence of peoples of European descent. (Turnbull-James, 2011)

It stands to reason therefore that these same theories inform educational leadership preparation programmes not only in the West but across many other parts of the globe including former colonies. Educational leadership preparation needs to evolve to better serve the Global Majority. Black leaders and other so-called minorities in sectors such as education often find that while they may agree that almost all successful leaders do indeed draw on a generic repertoire of basic human practices, leaders bring who they are by virtue of their backgrounds to how they approach the craft of leadership. This is a legitimate part of their professional identity. To exclude or deliberately not see leaders' background is to restrict the lens that leaders potentially bring through their lived experience to the leadership role. At a time when the communities that leaders serve are more diverse than ever, and the fault lines are exposed in the white-male Harvard-esque business model that is imploding, ignoring global leadership paradigms is not only tone-deaf and culturally illiterate, but the height of arrogance:

> 'There are some leadership practices intrinsic to the cultural backgrounds of Black and Global Majority peoples, that may not find their way into the mainstream cannons of western literature on leadership, such as the African concept of Ubuntu or Seva-centric leadership in the Asian tradition. The minoritisation of the group renders that which pertains to or comes from them, marginal' (Campbell-Stephens, 2009, p. 324)

The concept of Global Majority educators developing their capacity for leadership by working within their own cultural paradigms or indigenous knowledge and in so doing developing alternative narratives about under-achievement, equity, social justice, disengagement and moral purpose, as well as contributing to the theoretical thinking about leadership opens the way to explore how leadership preparation needs to be.

In addition, there is a preoccupation with leadership competences, traits and attributes; rarely are we invited to investigate their cultural roots, yet underlying values and roots they have. This has implications for those leaders who come from different cultures to those of the knowledge creators accredited by the academy. The unspoken pressure on leaders and those who teach them, is to assimilate to ways of seeing, being and doing that maintain the status quo. In fact, the degree to which your professionalism is recognised and your career progressed, can hinge on the degree to which you are seen as a conformist to the prevailing wisdom or dominant orthodoxy.

One thousand Black and other Global Majority teachers participated in Investing in Diversity a twelve-month leadership programme over eight years. As the developer and head of the programme, I was able to persuade a stellar cast of incredibly talented and committed tutors, to join an extraordinary team, including outstanding high-profile London Headteachers at the time. In some London boroughs, the numbers of Black senior and middle leaders doubled as a result of the various strands of the Investing in Diversity programme. Those Headteachers and Principals who could not tutor on the programme supported it in so many other ways, encouraging and supporting their Black and Asian staff to attend. In some schools there would be five or six members of staff attending from one school.

Most of the 1000 IiD participants in London came from the London Challenge boroughs, yet, inexplicably or perhaps predictably, race, Black epistemologies and the role that Black educators played in London Challenge's success were never acknowledged in any significant way as a contributory factor in the 'keys to success' identified in the literature. Black academics, educators, students and parents; their innovation; the role that the community played in supplementary schools, through mentoring projects; initiatives like Aiming High, another government programme this time run nationally with an all-Black team of consultants through the Department for Education; London schools and the Black Child conferences; the London Development Agency–commissioned research undertaken by Black researchers, all of these initiatives were running concurrently in London with the London Challenge and were never recognised or even referred to as a footnote within the London Challenge narrative, not seen, heard or cited. The prominent deficit narrative remained about under-representation of Black and Asian leaders at middle and senior leadership levels within London schools. What was implied or inferred by what was not said, is that there were insufficient numbers of Black and Asian teachers with the relevant experience or level of competence to put themselves forward for leadership. There was a conspiracy of silence about systemic racism that many Black, Asian and other Global Majority educators faced from the beginning of their careers to the end (Johnson & Campbell-Stephens, 2010; Coleman & Campbell-Stephens, 2010; Miller & Callender, 2019). In the keys to success narrative emerging from an analysis of the London Challenge initiative, London schools were dependent on white super heads to save them, some of whom had to be enticed out of retirement. We knew differently.

Investing in Diversity went on to inspire all the subsequent educational leadership programmes across England since 2003 focused on diversifying school leadership. There was not one such programme, whether Equal Access to Promotion, Diverse Leaders for Tomorrow or any of the myriad of others funded through the National College and subsequently directly from the Department for Education, focused on addressing BME under-representation that were not developed and/or led by tutors from the original Investing in Diversity Programme team.

As regards London Challenge, there was a wilful ignorance of, or arrogance towards Black educators' contribution to arguably the most successful government intervention to raise levels of attainment in the history of the British education system. While Black leadership was ignored, much was made about 'bringing in the right people' leading on a multi-million-pound initiative at the behest of the Prime Minister. The narrative of the largely white consultant heads, brought out of retirement to support leaders of struggling schools, under the leadership of the newly created post of London Schools Commissioner, was amplified in the literature:

> 'credible professionals to provide underperforming schools with the bespoke support they needed to improve while ensuring they were accountable to the department'. (Institute for Government, 2014, p4)

The irony and arrogance of this 'oversight' is incredulous, given the demographics of the London boroughs concerned. It demonstrated white supremacy in every aspect. Race was conspicuous by its absence in the

London Challenge narrative. Black students, parents and educators, including hundreds of teachers recruited from the Caribbean, were never even referred to within the epistemology that emerged from an initiative prefaced on the notion of partnership in one of the most racially diverse contexts on the planet. As we are reminded,

> there is a tradition that whiteness in educational research is sustained by the epistemological ignorance of race (Mills, 2007) and that European colonisation contributes to epistemcide, or the destruction of knowledge held by the subaltern.

Mills' seminal analysis of the 'epistemology of ignorance' can be summarised under what he describes as the five refusals of white supremacy; these are as follows:

> [A] refusal of the humanity of the other, a willingness to allow violence and exploitation to be inflicted. A refusal to listen to or acknowledge the experience of the other, resulting in marginalisation and active silencing. There is a refusal not just to confront long and violent histories of white domination, but to recognize how these continue to shape injustice into the present. There is a refusal to share space, particularly residential space, with resulting segregated geographies that perpetuate inequality and insulate white ignorance. Finally there is a refusal to face structural causes capitalism as it has intertwined with white supremacy from its earliest beginnings. (Gibson, 2018)

In addition, I would add that while the official line on eugenicist pseudo-science is that it is discredited, it is so deeply embedded in the foundations of white supremacist thinking and structures, that it will continue to inform policy decisions that impact detrimentally the people of the Global Majority. The refusals to see by the dominant structures extend to the refusal to see majority and minority status except to perpetuate the neo-liberal myth of (a) the Global Majority being 'minorities' and (b) the 'minorities' being responsible for the conditions in which they find themselves.

There is an urgent need to envision and reframe educational leadership discourse and praxis from a Global Majority perspective. The demographics in our cities and across the globe demand it. The academic leadership literature and leadership development practice should draw on the culturally relevant, social justice, equity focused, liberatory leadership work in

American contexts. While scholars like Miller and Callender (2019) and practitioners are adding to that field of knowledge through their work on anti-racism, diversity and inclusion in the UK, the literature about Black and Asian school leaders has largely focused on documenting the shortage of BME teachers and their failure to progress into senior leadership positions. It is time now in the UK to document Black conscious resistance to systemic racism from grass roots activity through to current academic scholarship across the full range of education from pre-school to professorship. Other peoples of the Global Majority are engaged in continuing the tradition of contextually and culturally rooting their indigenous knowledge, what Dei (2012) describes as 'heritage knowledge', across Asia, Africa, South America, the Caribbean, Australia and New Zealand, as well as the indigenous peoples of Canada and America. As we build our own institutions, scholarship and knowledge across the global south, we accumulate, learn about, share and pass on significant generational wealth through heritage knowledge.

Given the inequity embedded in our education systems globally, transformation has to be deliberate and intentionally embedded within leadership preparation. Education, in the interest of the greater good, moves beyond a narrow utilitarian role in economic development to the deeper questions of the kind of society that we are trying to build.

The State education systems that we have inherited were not envisioned to educate the working class, Black or poor; it is well documented that the schooling process was an industrial model intended to deliver a compliant workforce accepting of inequity as the norm, supported by the sifting and sorting mechanisms (assessments) at critical junctures in the process to deliver a basically schooled workforce and an educated elite. This system has outlived its usefulness in a transforming landscape. The transformation of our education systems in a Covid-19 world where we are striving to ensure that Black Lives Matter is dependent on the transformation of our thinking at all levels of the system.

Leadership preparation whether in London, Delhi or Kingston needs to be culturally literate, enabling people from diverse backgrounds to find their authentic voice, provide appropriate service and create different and inclusive culturally competent spaces for all. Issues around race and equity are particularly pressing, given that urban contexts globally are populated by Global Majority communities.

Models of educational leadership can no longer exist in a colour-blind, cultural or political vacuum; paradigms have to emerge out of their contexts and histories for a particular purpose in a given time. For Global Majority leaders to pursue their moral purpose will require more consensus about what their collective purpose is, an understanding of the historical legacy and the collective capacity to extract the politics from the policy direction as they build more equitable, just and therefore relevant and sustainable culturally competent organisations. Leadership preparation should acknowledge that we cannot simply 'graft' Black or Global Majority leaders on to processes and practices which are either diametrically opposed to where they are coming from culturally, or critically, not in their interests or that of the groups they represent, including their own children or grandchildren.

Developing a sense of personal agency is about being self-determining, not always responding to someone else's agenda, that is why assimilation is a difficult position for someone aware of their personal agency to take. Someone with agency has high levels of efficacy and awareness that one is initiating, executing and controlling one's own actions. Any leadership preparation programmes that we develop must embrace healing, and address trauma, as the toll of resistance to white supremacy is high, spiritually, intellectually, emotionally and physically.

Schools and the process of 'schooling' are among the most powerful tools we possess to socialise communities. They have the capacity to empower, nurture potential and release genius, or conversely to contain, control and arrest development. If we truly want education systems that address the needs of those groups that have historically been failed by them so that they can be healthy, happy and contributing citizens, leaders have to be transformational. All leaders of schools and children's services in any context need to have high levels of personal agency and in urban contexts that includes being culturally literate and especially competent in matters of race. Global Majority leaders have additionality beyond their pigmentation, and their capacity to act as role models to bring to this process.

The chapter ends therefore with a beginning. A global decolonising leadership movement that intentionally creates an alternative narrative, with the former 'colonised' as the beneficiaries; all the sweeter for having been first conceived in the heart of a former empire, on which it was claimed, the sun would never set.

# REFERENCES

Campbell-Stephens, R. (2009). Investing in diversity: changing the face (and the heart) of educational leadership. *School Leadership and Management, 29*(3), 321–331.

Coleman, M., & Campbell-Stephens, R. (2010). Perceptions of career progress: The experience of Black and Minority Ethnic school leaders. *School Leadership & Management, 30*(1), 35–49. https://doi.org/10.1080/13632430903509741

Dei, G. S. (2012). Indigenous anti-colonial knowledge as 'heritage knowledge' for promoting Black/African education in diasporic contexts. *Decolonization, Indigeneity, Education & Society, 1*(1), 102–119.

Gibson, A. (2018). The Five Refusals of White Supremacy. *American Journal of Economics and Sociology, 77*, 3–4.

Johnson, L., & Campbell-Stephens, R. (2010). Investing in Diversity in London Schools: Leadership Preparation for Black and Global Majority Educators. *Urban Education, 45*, 480.

Miller, P., & Callender, C. (2019). *Race, Education and Educational Leadership in England: An Integrated Analysis*. Bloomsbury Academic.

Mills, C. (2007). White ignorance. In *Race and Epistemologies of Ignorance* (pp. 11–38). State Univ of New York.

Turnbull-James, K. (2011). Leadership in context: Lessons from new leadership theory and current leadership development practice. The Kings fund.

# INDEX

© The Author(s), under exclusive license to Springer Nature
Switzerland AG 2021
R. M. Campbell-Stephens, *Educational Leadership and the Global
Majority*, https://doi.org/10.1007/978-3-030-88282-2

CPSIA information can be obtained
at www.ICGtesting.com
Printed in the USA
LVHW091757131221
706052LV00001B/30